NO LIMITS TO LOVE

Published alongside the premiere production by the Royal Shakespeare Company, *No Limits To Love* is the last stage play David Mercer wrote before his sudden death in August 1980.

Hugh, a history don at Oxford, Edward, a professional cellist, and Marna, Edward's wife, have set up an apparently amicable ménage à trois. All three commute between Edward's house in London and Hugh's in Oxford, but Edward has exclusive rights to Marna in London, while she is all Hugh's in Oxford.

They are in London when a new neighbour, Otto Neumann, moves into the house across the road. Otto, it turns out, has played a crucial role in the emotional life of both Edward and Hugh, and the impact he makes on the trio means that things can never be the same again . . . As David Mercer himself writes in a letter published as preface to the play, 'the people in *No Limits To Love* are grotesques; yet I would hope we might laugh and then reflect on the society in which their prototypes live out their stunted brief moment . . . I think I could convincingly argue that the play says a great deal about what people have become through the great social and economic disintegration of the Seventies.'

by the same author

AFTER HAGGERTY

THE BANKRUPT and other plays
  (The Bankrupt; You and Me and Him; Find Me; An Afternoon at the Festival)

COUSIN VLADIMIR and SHOOTING THE CHANDELIER

DUCK SONG

FLINT

THE GOVERNOR'S LADY

HUGGY BEAR and other plays
  (Huggy Bear; The Arcata Promise; A Superstition)

THE MONSTER OF KARLOVY VARY and THEN AND NOW

ON THE EVE OF PUBLICATION and other plays
  (On the Eve of Publication; The Cellar and the Almond Tree; Emma's Time)

David Mercer

No Limits TO LOVE

EYRE METHUEN · LONDON

First published in 1980 by Eyre Methuen Ltd
11 New Fetter Lane, London EC4P 4EE
Copyright © 1980 by the Estate of the late David Mercer
Set in IBM 10pt Journal by 𝄢 Tek-Art, Croydon, Surrey
Printed and bound in Great Britain by Whitstable Litho Ltd,
Whitstable, Kent

ISBN 0 413 48260 X

CAUTION
All rights whatsoever in this play are strictly reserved and
application for performance, etc., should be made before
rehearsal to Margaret Ramsay Ltd., 14a Goodwin's Court,
St. Martin's Lane, London WC2N 4LL. No performance may be
given unless a licence has been obtained.

To Rebecca

Preface

On 25 July 1980, just a fortnight before he died, David Mercer wrote to his publisher about No Limits To Love, *ruminating as to why it was that producers were — at the time he was writing — fighting shy of staging the play. What follows is an extract from that letter.* (Then and Now *is a stage play by Mercer first performed in 1979;* Let's Murder Vivaldi *is one of Mercer's television plays, first screened in 1968):*

Perhaps the play seems to have as little relation to the harsh realities of England now as *Design For Living* had in the Thirties. But I think this is to misunderstand it.

However, I think I could convincingly argue that it says a great deal about what people have become (natch I mean the middle-classes, I don't know any *real* workers!) through the great social and economic disintegration of the Seventies. Indeed in this respect it connects with the second act of *Then and Now;* and both plays were eerily prefigured by *Let's Murder Vivaldi.*

This is possibly because my central preoccupation in all three plays is the same: the increasing alienation of the 'modern consciousness' from the animal, poetic and symbolic sense of the unity of life at a more primitive stage of development. It sounds pretentious, I know. Also trite, as a theme. But what theme isn't? It hardly needs stating any more as an intellectual proposition that we have created a civilisation of unparalleled aridity; or rather that we are presiding over the confluence and decay of a number of cultures and might very possibly see the end of homo sapiens altogether, not to mention the rest of the 'innocent' life of this planet.

What we really need is a kind of Dickens of spiritual poverty and its causal mechanisms, someone (some, many-people) to charter the awful, deadening impact of our culture on human possibilities of spontaneity and feeling. The people in *No Limits*

To Love — with the exception maybe of Otto — are grotesques; yet I would hope we might laugh and then reflect on the society in which their prototypes live out their stunted brief moment. It may be I have contracted that peculiar disease authors are prone to, of seeing more in their own work than is actually there. All I know is what I am trying to do, insofar as I brood on my intentions in a general way at all. People don't seem to live out their lives in a 'true' connection with their emotions at all. The gulf between our archaic selves and our modern selves is awesome. We are cut off, trapped, shaped and self-shaped; and somehow the glorious creature that could be man (I imply nothing Rousseauesque) is like that wonderful line in the Donne poem: 'A great prince in prison lies'.

I think I am aiming at a 'comedy of absence' — and I mean the absence of the spiritual, the emotional, the aboriginal man. A rather grisly sort of comedy of what remains, but giving us the sensation of what has been lost . . . or perhaps never available since it was eliminated from us in childhood.

All of which, I must admit, sounds pretentious beyond belief.

Quand même, *No Limits To Love* could also come across as a mere 'entertainment' and I think might be justified on those grounds alone.

No Limits To Love was first presented by the Royal Shakespeare Company at the Warehouse Theatre, London on 2 October, 1980 with the following cast:

MARNA CROFT	Susan Tracy
EDWARD CROFT	Bob Peck
HUGH BAINBRIDGE	John Shrapnel
OTTO NEUMANN	Edward Petherbridge

Directed by Howard Davies
Designed by Sue Plummer
Lighting by Michael Calf

Act One

Scene One

The living-room of a house in North London. Late afternoon.
MARNA (late thirties) stands at the window looking out through
a pair of binoculars. EDWARD (early forties) enters with a paper.
He stands looking over her shoulder.

EDWARD. Settled in then, has he?

MARNA. Hello darling.

EDWARD. Removal men gone?

MARNA (*pecks his cheek*). Ages ago. Had a good day?

EDWARD. The usual.

MARNA. I think they were pissed out of their minds.

EDWARD. Went flying in the usual pile of dogshit by the front
   door. (*He sits*). Why me? Why always me?

   HUGH (*mid-forties*) *enters. He stands behind* MARNA. *He taps*
   the glasses.

HUGH. Naughty naughty.

MARNA. Hello darling.

HUGH. Moved in then, has he?

MARNA (*pecks his cheek*). This morning. Had a good day?

HUGH. Glummish. (*He sniffs: crosses to lift* EDWARD'S *foot.*)
   Thought so. How d'you do it? (*He drops the foot and goes for*
   a drink.)

EDWARD. Why never you? Why never her?

HUGH. Well. For one thing. Marna and I don't walk about as if
   recently lobotomised. Do we?

MARNA (*still with the glasses*). I think our new neighbour's a bit pissed as well. There seems to be only him.

HUGH. Awful business, moving in.

MARNA. He's sitting on the lav drinking whisky straight from the bottle.

EDWARD. It's disgusting of you to stand there watching a man crap.

MARNA. I don't think he is.

HUGH. You used to watch the Denhams.

EDWARD. The Denhams were fascists.

MARNA. He's rather beautiful.

EDWARD. He's what?

MARNA. He's got the most fascinating face. (*Pause*.) Bony. Lined. Sort of philosophical.

EDWARD. Remember how Denham used to wipe his arse standing up? (*Pause*.) Quirky. Something amiss there.

MARNA. Short iron-grey hair. Lovely hands.

EDWARD. I expect the removal men didn't unpack his glasses. I'd like to think it's that. I couldn't stand another one right opposite.

HUGH. Another what?

EDWARD. Drunk. We've got two in this street already.

MARNA. Don't be paranoid Edward.

EDWARD. What's paranoia? Just a clinical term for a heightened sense of proportion.

MARNA (*to* EDWARD). Want a peek?

EDWARD. No thanks. I refuse to pass judgement on a crapping human.

MARNA (*gives the glasses to* HUGH). You did on the Denhams. Till she put the curtain up.

EDWARD. That was research. It's a well-known fact that when anal fixation becomes endemic it can lead to a right-wing putsch.

HUGH. He's definitely not crapping though. (*Pause*.) Could it be endemic?

EDWARD. It was over there. He was Hitler. She was Goering. And those horrific children were Roehm, Heidrich and Himmler respectively.

MARNA. I quite liked Sheila.

EDWARD. It also leads to conspicuous meanness. What do you make of a woman who moves out taking the lavatory curtain with her?

HUGH. Denham used to knock it back in the loo, you know. Kept a half-bottle in that thing where you put the brush. (*He puts the glasses down.*) So much for socialism.

EDWARD. What?

HUGH. Yes. You'd naturally be ignorant of the fact that he was a Labour Councillor. How long have you had this house is it?

EDWARD. Twelve, thirteen years.

HUGH. Yes and you've had Marna around for ten. She seems to know everybody. What's the matter with you?

EDWARD. Funny way to talk about marriage. Having somebody around.

HUGH (*as* EDWARD *drifts to the window*). I always get the impression that's the way you look at it yourself.

EDWARD (*looking out*). I was alone when I moved in here. No carpets. No furniture. (*Pause.*) Girl I knew — Polly something or other — used to sit there. On that very spot. On the bare floor. Drinking champagne all day and playing 'Bridge Over Troubled Waters'. (*Pause.*) What a golden summer that was. Wild. Way out. (*Pause.*) I believe Marna was assisting in one of those abortive French revolutions at the time.

MARNA. I wouldn't put it quite like that.

EDWARD. Yes you were. I saw you on a barricade. (*Firmly to* HUGH:) In Paris. She was a kind of ideological groupie in those days. Absolutely in her element digging up cobblestones.

MARNA. I took some medical supplies over, that's all.

EDWARD. Yes. So you did. Considering all the pharmacies were open at the time I thought it very eccentric of you.

HUGH. What were you doing in Paris at the time?

EDWARD. Just passing through. I was always passing through places where Marna was in those days. She never seemed to recognise me. Too busy sucking up to that dazzling demagogue she was keen on. What was his name, that Belgian one? They all seemed to be called Schwartzbart-Outré or something of the sort. (*Pause*.) You'd think at least the cello case would have rung a bell.

HUGH. Do you make a habit of it?

EDWARD. What?

HUGH. Humping your cello through abortive revolutions.

EDWARD. You can sneer. I have a strong suspicion she didn't recognise me the day we got married either.

MARNA. He was beautiful.

HUGH. When you got married? Edward was?

MARNA. My Belgian.

EDWARD (*at the window with the glasses: he sings*). Like a bridge over trou-houbled waters, I shall lay me down —

HUGH. Where is she now?

EDWARD. Who?

HUGH. Polly something-or-other.

EDWARD. Not my province.

HUGH. What isn't?

EDWARD. Where Polly is isn't. (*Pause*.) Schwartzers, I'm relieved to say. Is locked up. In Paraguay is it?

MARNA. Peru.

EDWARD. One of those countries.

MARNA *is quietly but unmistakeably in tears.* HUGH *goes to put his arms round her.*

HUGH. There, Marnie —

MARNA. He's always so vile about Jean-Jacques.

EDWARD. It isn't as if they shot him or anything. What's fifteen years when he can take all those correspondence courses?

HUGH. Pretty grim though, these Latin American nicks.

EDWARD. Any regime that put old J.J. away for fifteen years

deserves the Nobel Peace Prize.

HUGH. Knew him well, did you?

EDWARD. Never actually ran across him. (*Pause.*) I do know he fancied himself a bit of a poet. That's the way to Marna's heart sure enough. (*Pause.*) I could fart hexameters better than he could write them.

MARNA. Stop it!

EDWARD (*proffers the glasses to* HUGH). Care for another gander?

HUGH. I think it's time you packed in the binoculars bit.

EDWARD. Time *I* did!

HUGH. We don't make a habit of it. It was you Gerry Denham threatened to prosecute. Did I spy on him and Sheila? Did Marna?

EDWARD. That's a bit hard. Research not spying, you know.

HUGH. Sheila told Marna. He didn't give a shit if you watched him crapping. Not after Korea.

EDWARD. What?

HUGH. It was your goggling at Sheila had him rattled.

EDWARD. Well. If I'd known he'd been in Korea.

HUGH. Won a medal.

EDWARD. Which side was he on?

HUGH. Seems they had a twenty-eight holer at Pyongyang.

MARNA (*firmly to* EDWARD). I think it might be just as well if you stayed in London this weekend.

Pause.

EDWARD. I was looking forward to Oxford.

MARNA. I think we could do without you for a few days.

HUGH. I could do without him altogether.

EDWARD. It's what we agreed. I'm entitled to go. I have a right to the same number of days in Oxford as he has in London.

MARNA. You think I was in a bad way when you picked up the pieces after Jean-Jacques? Tell him, Hugh. Tell him what a mess I was in when we met you.

HUGH. I'll say. Well on the way to the funny-farm old son.

EDWARD. Now you've destroyed me. (*Pause*.) I'd been feeling quite chipper. We played the Schubert E flat this afternoon and really — really I was out of this world. You know that Swedish folk-theme in the andante? I absolutely took off. (*Pause: musing*.) Flipping her lid, was she? Blow me down.

MARNA. That's something else I can do without.

EDWARD. What is?

MARNA. Damn it — cut it out will you?

EDWARD. Cut what out?

HUGH. I think she means, Edward. She means this persistent affectation of yours that you've no idea what people are talking about.

EDWARD. What people?

MARNA. I shall go mad. I swear I shall.

EDWARD. Funny woman. Been semi-yo-yo all her life though if you ask me. Did she tell you I once saved it? On the beach at Southwold. Tried to drown herself.

HUGH. You rescued her?

EDWARD. Christ no, I can't swim. But the bloke that did was kneeling there on the sand trying to pump the water out of her lungs. He gave up after a bit and when I remonstrated he yelled: who the hell are you? (*Pause*.) I don't know what came over me, but I said: that's my future wife you've got on her back between your knees.

　　Pause.

HUGH. You mean the prospect of being married to you actually brought her to life? Brought her soul scampering back from the gates of paradise?

EDWARD. That's right. Because when she heard the news she threw up and started breathing.

HUGH. How extraordinary.

MARNA. Edward —

EDWARD. We put the banns up the following week. (*Pause*.) Aren't we going to the theatre tonight?

MARNA. Were you looking forward to it?

EDWARD. Straining at the leash. Did you get the tickets?

MARNA *finds three tickets in her handbag. She tears one of them into small pieces and throws them in* EDWARD'S *face. She goes out.*

EDWARD *crouches to pick up the pieces.* HUGH *looks on, filling a pipe.*

HUGH. Seems a pity.

EDWARD. Not if it's anything like the last play we saw.

HUGH. Which was that?

EDWARD. Bent copper buggering a pregnant cripple in a block of highrise flats.

HUGH. Why was he doing that?

EDWARD. Capitalism. (*Pause.*) End of the first act they took off up the M1 in her disabled person's three-wheeler to dynamite a nuclear power station.

HUGH. I remember. (*Pause.*) But for the life of me I still don't know why they were all bald in the second act.

EDWARD. Malnutrition. The bent copper's fascist-abortionist mother became Prime Minister and turned England into one bloody big Auschwitz. Some good bits in the programme though.

HUGH. Such as?

EDWARD. Haircuts by Vidal Sassoon.

Pause.

HUGH. What I was trying to get at before. Is it's a pity about our modus vivendi. Slow attrition of.

EDWARD. The what of our what?

HUGH. There you go again, you see. That's it precisely. This wilful obtuseness you've been going in for lately. (*Pause.*) Driving Marna and me up the wall.

EDWARD. Of course in my racket we have things like 'andante cantabile'. 'Con fuoco'. 'Allegro rallentando'. And so on. But your average cellist doesn't walk round shoving them into ordinary conversations.

HUGH. I think you've gone sour on the whole thing and you're beginning to take it out on us.

EDWARD. I know a fiddler in the LSO who wouldn't know attrition from constipation

HUGH. Aggression I can take. What I can't stand is people disowning it.

EDWARD. I'm not disowning it. For instance I very nearly scraped that dogshit off with your toothbrush.

HUGH. There now. That didn't hurt — did it?

EDWARD. What?

HUGH. Talking it through. Instead of doing it.

EDWARD. I did scrape it off on Marna's.

HUGH. You didn't.

EDWARD. I did.

HUGH. That takes us right back to square one. (*Rising*.) You filthy bastard.

EDWARD. Yes. Awful to think it could be the real me.

HUGH (*crosses to door shouting*). Marna —

MARNA *enters, pushing past him with a toothbrush. She waves it under* EDWARD'S *nose.*

MARNA. So what about this?

EDWARD. Shall we talk it through?

MARNA. I very nearly used it before I caught the pong.

EDWARD. You never used to brush your teeth before you went to the theatre with me.

MARNA. What's that you're chewing? You know I can't bear it.

EDWARD. I'm not chewing.

MARNA. Yes you are. Open up. Let me see.

He does so. She rams the toothbrush in his mouth. EDWARD goes out spluttering.

HUGH. I say, Marna.

MARNA. What?

HUGH. I don't think you've quite got the principle.

MARNA. Of what?

HUGH. The triumph of reason over impulse.

MARNA. Oh. That.

HUGH. I don't think either of you's got the hang of it.

MARNA. He's a lunatic.

HUGH. Steady on.

MARNA. An act of calculated malice is not an impulse.

HUGH. Agreed. But you lose out if you react.

MARNA. I mean — he's the one who's supposed to be inhibited. Right?

HUGH. Frankly, I think it was cruel of you to marry him.

MARNA. You also think it would be cruel of me to divorce him.

HUGH. I don't think either of you could live with it. What he hasn't grasped yet is. That if you love someone as much as he loves you, well you just have to ride the blows. Struggle for detachment. I told him. 'Edward', I said. 'Flexibility is the hallmark of an altruistic passion.'

MARNA. And what about integrity?

HUGH. Quite. That's exactly what we need. Flexible integrity. (*Pause*.) Mind you. One has to say it. Not much passion kicking about inside the chap to begin with. Is there?

MARNA. I'll not have you run him down behind his back. I thought we agreed that from the start.

HUGH. You know what Marnie?

MARNA. What?

HUGH. If you don't pull yourself together. You'll drive him and me both up the wall.

Pause.

MARNA. I do feel ashamed about tearing up his wretched ticket.

HUGH. Very self-indulgent of you.

Pause.

MARNA. You'll never understand what it is between Edward and me.

HUGH. On the contrary. If I didn't appreciate how deeply you care for each other I'd be off like a shot.

Pause.

MARNA. He was beautiful. In a way.

HUGH. On the beach at Southwold?

MARNA. Oh I'd decided to marry him long before that. I'm a terrific swimmer. What I didn't know at the time was he had this phobia about water.

HUGH. Among so many. He went crazy when a ladybird landed on his toast this morning.

MARNA. But he was so patient when I was going through the Jean-Jacques thing. I nearly went to Peru after him in sixty-nine you know.

HUGH. Beastly decade, the sixties. One of my students wanted to burn all the books. What — another Reichstag? I said. Another what? he said. (*Pause.*) They did seem to despise one so unremittingly.

MARNA. I came to realise how devoted he was to me. Truly selfless.

HUGH. Yes. Astonishing. Soon as I clapped eyes on Edward I thought: 'Now there's a chap who can put across sheer unbridled egoism as genuine humility.'

MARNA. Don't, Hugh. He tries awfully hard. (*Pause.*) I grew to love him and I always shall.

HUGH. And me?

MARNA (*crosses to him*). I adore you.

HUGH. I love your hair like that. You've got such a sweet neck.

MARNA. Nuzzle me.

HUGH (*kisses her neck*). All the same. It was a bit thick stuffing the brush in his mouth.

MARNA *giggles.*

He didn't seem to find it screamingly funny.

MARNA. Oh come on. I wouldn't dream of being so vicious. It was a new brush dipped in marmite.

HUGH (*kisses her neck*). Coward. Still. It was a very ugly trick on his part. I wonder if being Edward is worse than knowing him? (*He licks her ear.*)

MARNA. That's lovely. (*Pause.*) I'm glad my neck drives you round the bend. If it does.

HUGH. Bonkers. Horny as an armadillo.

MARNA. Ah-ah. Not till Oxford.

HUGH. You know that's the only part of the arrangement I don't much care for. I mean it goes without saying. There are times when I want you very much in London. Just as he must when we're in Oxford.

MARNA, Those were the terms. We all promised. Your roof is your roof and his roof is his roof.

HUGH (*to the ceiling*). Rather a waste of a good roof.

MARNA. No. I couldn't bear it. I respect him too much.

HUGH. Sensitive old thing.

MARNA. I do care about his feelings.

HUGH. That's the spirit. (*Pause.*) It gets damned urgent some nights though. Could almost carry you off whilst he's asleep and have you down here. Right there where Polly used to drink champagne. (*Sings.*) I will lay me down —

MARNA. Please, Hugh.

HUGH (*embracing her*). I know. You'd be rushing up every five minutes to see if he was wincing. He does a lot of that. Muriel was a bit of a wincer, come to think of it. (*Pause.*) Barbarous little bitch.

MARNA (*breaking away*). How is she?

HUGH. No idea.

MARNA. You mean you've stopped visiting her?

HUGH. Not much point with a catatonic. Is there?

MARNA. That's not funny.

HUGH. It wasn't meant to be. It's just literally true.

MARNA. My blood froze for a second.

HUGH. It wasn't funny being married to her either.

MARNA. So why were you?

Pause.

HUGH. Caught me on the rebound. I'd been wildly in love with somebody else. Lucky escape that was. Otherwise trapped for life with someone who couldn't distinguish between passion and hysteria.

Pause.

MARNA. I think we've both had a rough time. One way or another.

HUGH. I'm a bit touchy on the subject of Muriel, you see.

MARNA. I'm sorry.

HUGH. You needn't be. She conned me all right. I'd thought she was just averagely awful. Averagely rotten and evil. How was I to know she'd turn out a genuine lunatic? (*Pause.*) Just when I thought I'd got life decently organised round a twisted mind, she ups and overrides the moral categories by getting certified. (*Pause.*) What a triumph.

MARNA. Well. Edward's organised his life around my lovers. D'you think he'd be reassured if I were classified a nymphomaniac?

HUGH. Might be more human if he showed a bit more spark.

MARNA. Ah. But when he does — all he gets is a lecture from you.

Pause.

HUGH. Which way do you want him and me to jump, Marna?

MARNA. I've learned not to have very high expectations of emotional cripples. (*Crossing to the door.*) Time we were off.

She goes out. HUGH *goes to the window and looks out with the glasses.*

HUGH. Well well well. (*Pause.*) Otto Neumann. (*He goes.*)

Blackout.

Fade in:

Scene Two:

Later the same evening. EDWARD — *in a dressing-gown over shirt and trousers — sprawls in a chair with a music score listening to a classical concert on the radio.*

The doorbell rings. And again after a moment.

EDWARD *goes out and returns with the man from across the road —* OTTO NEUMANN. OTTO *is much as described by* MARNA *and very spruce in a dark suit, shirt and tie. He stands looking round the room as* EDWARD *switches off the radio.*

OTTO. I didn't wish to disturb you Edward. What a beautiful house.

EDWARD. Marna's taste. My wife. She put it together over the years. Says you have to let a place grow. (*Looking round.*) In fact the only thing of mine in here's that Nigerian mask. Did a concert in Lagos way back.

OTTO. So you still play professionally?

EDWARD. Oh yes. (*Pause.*) Probably tourist junk. Powerful though — aren't they?

OTTO. A mask — is a mask.

EDWARD. I'd forgotten you're something of an expert.

OTTO. I hope you don't mind my dropping in on you like this. I saw the others go out earlier. (*Pause.*) It seemed a good moment perhaps to find you alone. (*Pause.*) An impulse.

EDWARD. Lord no. Quite knocked me out seeing you there at the door. How are you Dr Neumann?

OTTO. You never did manage to call me Otto, did you? (*Pause.*) But I'd appreciate it if you would now.

EDWARD. What about a drink?

OTTO. Thank you. A scotch and water if I may.

EDWARD (*getting the drink*). Couldn't believe my eyes.

OTTO. I should say at once. I noticed you all watching this afternoon. One after the other.

EDWARD. Sorry about that. Nasty habit. I didn't get on with your predecessor.

OTTO. Did you know him well?

EDWARD. Never actually met him. But he had an amazing excretory routine. Picked it up in Korea, it seems. (*He brings the drink and a tonic for himself*.) I am sorry. You know how it is. A new chap moves in. We were intrigued and so on.

OTTO. Denham, was it? Gerald Denham?

EDWARD. Don't tell me you know him.

OTTO. No. But he leased the house from my sister.

EDWARD. I thought you were in Canada.

OTTO. I was, yes. I have been there until recently. (*Pause*.) Frieda died two years ago and left me that house. When my lawyer wrote and told me the lease had come up and Denham didn't wish to renew . . . how shall I put it? I had a sudden overwhelming nostalgia for Europe. And here I am. (*Pause*.) Perhaps you didn't recognise me?

Pause.

EDWARD. Well I did, as a matter of fact.

OTTO. Cheers. (*He drinks*.)

EDWARD. Cheers.

Pause.

OTTO. If I have embarrassed you —

EDWARD. Not at all. Quiet evening at home, you know. Spot of Bartok on the radio. Took me years to get the hang of Bartok. Should be at the theatre with Marna really. But I couldn't face it.

OTTO. It's very good to see you, Edward.

EDWARD. I never managed the Elgar concerto. Remember the tussle we had about Elgar? (*Pause*.) I was never given the chance, actually.

Pause.

OTTO. I went to a concert your trio gave in Montreal. Sixty-five would it be? (*Pause*.) Koenig violin? Yes Koenig. And a beautiful young lady whose name I cannot remember, at the piano.

EDWARD. Polly Koenig. Hans's cousin. (*Pause*.) If I'd had any sense I'd have married Polly. But was stuck on Marna. Always, really.

OTTO. Such a long time ago. But I do remember you played the Schubert E flat most thrillingly.

EDWARD. Odd, that. I played it today. Not with the krauts, though. We parted company in sixty-eight. (*Pause*.) You might have come round, in Montreal. Said hello. (*Pause*.) We could have had a meal. You like champagne — you'd have loved Polly. (*Pause*.) I think I did once wring it out of you that you liked champagne.

OTTO. I was very unhappy during those days.

EDWARD. We might have cheered you up. Got to know you a bit. Would it have been unethical or something?

OTTO. Of course not.

EDWARD. I used to think. When I got up off your couch and went out. Used to wonder if you somehow ceased to exist. (*Pause*.) Or if I did.

OTTO. I recall we did a lot of useful work on that one Edward.

Pause.

EDWARD. So we did.

OTTO. As a matter of fact that concert was my last evening with someone I was very fond of. A rather bitter and very sad occasion. He was flying back to London the same night.

EDWARD. You're looking well.

OTTO. And so do you.

EDWARD. I really am sorry about all that with the binoculars.

OTTO. D'you remember what I used to say about your chronic apologising?

EDWARD. You quit when I was just getting into the swing of it.

OTTO. We learn that the sky will not fall. When we do something others disapprove of.

EDWARD. Yes. Well. I always thought that sounded a bit sanctimonious.

OTTO. Did you tell your wife you know me?

EDWARD. I don't know you.

OTTO. I didn't exactly quit. You knew I left for Canada for the most compelling personal reasons.

EDWARD. The kind some of us came to you for in the first place?

OTTO. I'm sorry we hadn't got further when I went.

EDWARD. You might have walked away out of sheer cracking boredom. I thought at the time.

OTTO. So Bernard Glossop told me. He wrote that you stormed out one day and never went back.

EDWARD. He was insensitive and mediocre.

OTTO. Shall we say he had another style. Another approach. It was a mistake passing you on to him, I agree. (*He smiles.*) You had a fantasy that your analyst should be incapable of mistakes. Did you not?

Pause.

EDWARD. Could we have got any further?

OTTO. What do you think?

EDWARD. I think — it's academic now.

OTTO. But isn't this progress? You regained distinction in your music. You have a most attractive wife. A lovely house. (*Pause.*) Are there children?

EDWARD. No.

OTTO. It can still be.

EDWARD. She's pushing forty. You're beginning to sound like Glossop. When did you take to boozing in the lavatory?

OTTO. Dear me. The ageing analyst has feet of clay and his nose in a bottle too?

EDWARD. Hard to believe I ever stood in awe of you. Or lay, rather. (*Pause.*) I tried to bully Glossop into having that broken spring in the couch mended. You can imagine the kind of session we had about the significance of resenting a coiled spring up your arse. D'you know he didn't even bother to redecorate the place after you left? And instead of those linen napkins you used to put on the pillow, it was Kleenex with him. Must have been a week at least before I realised I was walking out each day with a tissue stuck to the back of my head. (*Pause.*) I could forgive all if you've turned into an alcoholic.

OTTO. No. I thought the removal men had lost my Kokoschka drawing today. Where did I find it? Mysteriously tucked away behind the lavatory basin. So it was a celebration your wife was observing. Kokoschka and Neumann united once more, in the scheisshaus. Alas they had not unpacked my glasses. So I must drink from the bottle. Will that do?

EDWARD. Ingenious — if implausible.

OTTO. But it's true. (*Pause*.) May I ask — who was the other man?

EDWARD. You know that photo you had of your father on a walking tour with Jung in the Tyrol?

OTTO. I still have it.

EDWARD. Well. In the light patch on the wallpaper so recently vacated by the two grand old men. Dr Bernard C. Glossop hung a small nasty picture of his baby daughter. Had a bubble of snot coming out of one nostril, which he thought a very whimsical touch.

OTTO. My dear fellow — I don't feel responsible for him.

EDWARD. But how could you hand me over to such a cretin?

Pause.

OTTO. In any case. I ceased to practice as an analyst about the time you were in Montreal. Do you still regard it as unfinished business?

EDWARD. I'm perfectly all right, thanks.

OTTO. Are you?

EDWARD. Really. I'm fine. (*Pause*.) Finally caught on it's all a load of bollocks did you? Oh dear. Didn't mean that did I? (*Pause*.) It's very confusing having you turn up like this, you know. Pity you've given it up. We could have had a ball on the theme of the return of the prodigal analyst.

Pause.

OTTO. I went back into general practice. Out in the wilds. (*Pause*.) Appendixes. Births. Broken limbs. Frostbite. Preventive medicine. (*Pause*.) I needed to learn how to be completely self-sufficient. (*Pause*.) How to be alone.

EDWARD. I'd say why? But the drill was, you always turned

personal questions back on me. If I remember rightly. Wasn't that part of the technique?

OTTO. Have you begun to feel like a patient again? As if the intervening years had not happened?

EDWARD. Christ no.

OTTO. This can happen.

EDWARD. No. I feel fine.

OTTO. I'm glad.

EDWARD. What took me by surprise though —

Pause.

OTTO. Yes?

EDWARD. As soon as I saw you again tonight. I knew you're someone I'd absolutely trust. Always. (*Pause.*) I don't know anything about you as a person. But I felt that. (*Pause.*) I think I'd like to know you as a friend.

OTTO. I hope you will. And I hope I can live down my defection, too. (*Pause.*) I'm very touched, Edward.

EDWARD. There you stood at the door. And — I was happy to see you. A real gush of warmth. (*Pause.*) I very nearly cried.

Pause.

OTTO. As you never did when you were my patient.

Pause.

EDWARD. I did hate you when you went away. But the panic attacks became fewer and further between. (*Pause.*) I thought: 'Whatever else — there's a great deal to be panic-stricken about.' (*Pause.*) But I also think now, that people who feel unforgiven have quite a tolerance for losing out. (*He grins.*) D'you remember that old crack of yours about necessity being the invention of mother?

Pause.

OTTO. Unforgiven — did you say?

Pause.

EDWARD. Yes. Well. We're not going back to all that. Are we?

OTTO *crosses to the window and looks out. He finds the Nigerian mask. He picks it up.*

OTTO. It was a young man I went to Canada for. And alas it was him I was putting on the plane to London the night of your concert. (*Pause*.) Of course I did not tell him this remarkable cellist is once my patient. (*Pause*.) I thought the Schubert E flat a most poignant way of saying auf wiedersehen to Rinaldo. (*He puts the mask down*.) He was so charming. And a great deal more besides. He had restored my delight in the simplest things of life. (*Pause*.) He received one's most foolish and embarrassing impulses with a kind of grace. (*He smiles gently*.) Also he left me quite gracefully, too.

Pause. A door slams.

EDWARD. That'll be Marna. Er, and Hugh of course. That's his name, the other chap. History don at Oxford. Fellow and all that. Oriel, would it be? Or Magdelen? Or am I in Cambridge? (*Pause*.) Yes. Well this place is more or less his London pied-à-terre. More like pied-à-dogshit you may have noticed. Useful arrangement all round. One foot in Oxford. One in the metropolis. And Otto —

OTTO. I should pause for breath if I were you.

EDWARD. I didn't tell them I know you.

OTTO. I take it you don't wish me to hide in a cupboard, or something of the kind?

EDWARD. If you don't stand by me I shall blow your cover. Hugh can be very nasty about psychoanalysis. It's a mean little pose but he dines with people who understand linguistic philosophy and so forth. Seems they're very standoffish about the life of the mind.

OTTO. Do calm down, Edward. I myself begin to feel as if you got up off my couch only yesterday.

EDWARD. I'm fine, fine. They're a fascinating couple.

OTTO. Which of them frightens you most — your wife? Or — if you'll pardon the insight — her lover?

EDWARD. Insight be damned. I'll bet you watched him squeezing her arse all the way to my car.

OTTO. I assure you I did not. However. So we are shoulder to shoulder. But then may I have another whisky?

EDWARD *takes his glass to refill it*. MARNA *and* HUGH *enter*.

MARNA. Hello —

EDWARD. Marna this is Otto Neumann. Otto — Marna, my wife. And Hugh Bainbridge.

They shake hands.

MARNA. From over the road?

OTTO. Yes indeed.

MARNA. You know each other?

OTTO. We were acquainted — oh, very many years ago.

EDWARD. Yes. Well he's been in Canada ever since. Rubbing shoulders with the moose. The caribou. Mounties and all that.

MARNA. Are you a musician?

OTTO. A mere sawbones, Mrs Croft. Not so much a flying doctor but — so to speak — a flown one. My practice covered many hundreds of square miles. Forests. Mountains. Lakes.

MARNA. Those awful traps.

OTTO. I beg your pardon?

MARNA. Those bear traps. I have nightmares about them.

HUGH. Ever get called in to a bear?

He and OTTO *are eyeing each other warily.* MARNA *goes on without noticing.*

MARNA. Very odd of you not to mention it Edward. That you'd met before. (*To* OTTO *as she gets a drink*:) I mean we've all been staring across the road like mad. Wondering who. It's very rude, of course. But something of an event, a new neighbour. Pretty much a backwater I'm afraid. Near-geriatrics mostly. One of the few really villagey places still left in central London. Edward worked it out once. If they drop a Hiroshima-sized bomb on the House of Commons, we're just outside the radius of instant vapourisation. Spends a lot of time making calculations of that sort. I think he's of the opinion that God got bored with things after Mahler died. (HUGH *is staring at* OTTO *again.*) Don't tell me you and Hugh know each other as well.

OTTO. My father knew Mahler. But Mr Bainbridge and I have never met, I think. Forgive me. I was not staring at you

Mr Bainbridge. I was thinking of my house over there. So inhospitable at the monent.

MARNA. Was he really an absolute shithouse?

OTTO. I beg your pardon?

MARNA. Mahler. Did he ever dandle you on his knee?

OTTO. I am not quite so old, Mrs Croft. But my mother was in Heiligenstadt when he died. Alma Mahler went up there to the Hohe Warte. She told my mother he believed himself conducting Mozart when he was dying.

HUGH. They can't bite the dust soon enough, for my money.

OTTO. Who cannot?

HUGH. Musicians in any shape or form. (*He yawns.*) Saving your presence, Edward. Got to be exceptions, haven't there? I'd confess I hate art altogether, really. But Marna says that's the sort of posture that dates one. All I can say is my students got pretty snotty about art in the sixties, and one does try to keep up. Different atmosphere altogether in the seventies. I will say for recessions, they have a remarkably sobering effect on the student population. I'm off to bed if you'll all excuse me. (*He pecks* MARNA'S *cheek*.) Nighty-nighty. (*He pats* EDWARD'S *head*.) Sleepy-tighty. (*He bows to* OTTO.) Ciao, Dottore. (He *goes*.)

Pause.

EDWARD. You'd think a fool like that would be debarred from expressing any opinions whatsoever on history.

MARNA. Don't, Edward. I've got such a headache.

OTTO. I must be off too, Mrs Croft.

MARNA. Marna.

OTTO. It has been a pleasure to meet you. To realise that after all one is not completely among strangers.

MARNA. That's a lot of house for somebody all alone. Why don't you come to lunch tomorrow if you're free?

OTTO. I am, and I will. Thank you. You are most kind. (*Going.*) Goodnight, Edward.

EDWARD. 'Night.

OTTO *is followed out by* MARNA. EDWARD *switches on the*

radio and settles in a chair. MARNA *enters and switches the* *radio off.*

MARNA. Why weren't we letting on, then?

EDWARD. Just a chap I ran across once or twice in the early sixties. The decade of the death of art.

MARNA. Don't Edward. (*She sits, holding her head.*)

EDWARD. He wasn't grey then. He was quite plump, as well. I wouldn't have thought he'd ever get to look so frail. (*Pause.*) An acquaintance, that's all.

MARNA. You could have seen him out yourself.

EDWARD. I can't compete with the way you suck up to new people.

MARNA (*rising*). I'm off to bed.

EDWARD (*rising*). Me too, then.

MARNA (*sits*). If things are not working out for you we'll have it out. You know how dreamy I get in the bathroom. I didn't even look at the bloody toothbrush till I started to squeeze the paste on. What you'd done came to me in a flash. A complete and total vision of it right down to the last detail.

EDWARD (*sits*). Marna —

MARNA. A gestalt. An epiphany. A revelation.

EDWARD. Marna —

MARNA. When I saw that filthy brown mess on the brush —

EDWARD. Don't you remember that awful sort of ersatz Bovril I brought back when we did a concert in Warsaw?

Pause.

MARNA. Oh.

EDWARD. How it stank like the doggy minefield out there?

MARNA. Caught again, Marna.

EDWARD. I was touched though you know, by your Marmite. When I got over the shock. When I realised. Laughed so much I nearly keeled over. Took me back to the old days.

MARNA. It did? Yes. Well. The early stages of our relationship were not so much intimate as infantile. It might even have been more mature if you'd had the guts to use real dogshit.

EDWARD. Wouldn't that have been heretical? Given the gospel according to St Hugh?

MARNA. Well he's right, isn't he? If you're going to bottle up your aggression then take refuge in these silly little childish campaigns. We all three come out of it badly.

Pause.

EDWARD. I saw Tom Weatherby in a pub today when I popped in for a beer and a sandwich. Remember Tom? Philharmonia? Flute and piccolo?

MARNA. No.

EDWARD. 'There he goes', I heard him say to his friends. 'Poor old Eddie Croft. Your original square on the hypotenuse of the eternal triangle.'

A pause. MARNA crosses to kneel in front of him. She rests her head on his thigh.

MARNA. Oh, Edward. Dearest Edward. I couldn't bear to lose you though.

EDWARD. Nor I you.

MARNA. We still have everything that's precious. Everything we had before.

EDWARD. Yes. All that and Hugh on top. Ought to thank our lucky stars, really. (*Pause.*) If he and Muriel weren't divorced I wonder how she and I'd have hit it off. (*Pause.*) Did she go insane before or after they split up?

MARNA (*moves away*). I refuse to discuss it when Hugh's not here.

EDWARD. To defend himself?

MARNA. Stop it, will you?

EDWARD. Who started it? Who lay in the bath one day when I was shaving. And informed me as I quietly slashed my face to ribbons. That we either incorporate Hugh Bainbridge into our lives or get a divorce?

MARNA. Oh yes. The day after — may I remind you? — the day after you pretended to have an epileptic fit when he took you in to dinner at High Table.

EDWARD. What did we have before, by the way? (*Pause.*) In the beginning. (*Pause*.) We all know my role after Schwartzbart-Farouche was to provide you with a stable environment till you found someone else to go beserk with. And I've watched some pretty exotic failures come and go in the past ten years. But why that ignominious fart upstairs? For one thing he's almost exactly like me. (*Rising*.) I'm going to bed.

MARNA (*rising*). I think that's a very good idea. You and I never exactly went berserk — did we?

Pause.

EDWARD (*sits*). I was your refuge, you said.

Pause.

MARNA. You were and you are.

EDWARD. Your very best friend.

MARNA. It's true.

EDWARD. This house a small circle of light and warmth. A cave. (*Pause*.) Whilst the final storms gather outside.

Pause.

MARNA. It is.

Pause.

EDWARD. Old Schwartzers would have wiped the floor with you.

MARNA (*sits*). That's better.

EDWARD. What is?

MARNA. Aren't you really edging close to saying you'd like to wipe the floor with me yourself?

EDWARD. Am I?

MARNA. Of course. Which is precisely what Hugh and I are always trying to reassure you about.

EDWARD. You mean I'm beginning to get the hang of it?

MARNA. Right. Once you can admit in so many words but without actually having to do it. Then you've exorcised the impulse.

Pause.

EDWARD. What nags me though. Is how you reconcile that with

the way you both drivel on about the need for spontaneity.

MARNA (*rising*). I really am going up this time.

EDWARD (*rising*). When we're all in London —

MARNA. What?

EDWARD. Do you ever get out of our bed during the night and come down here to make love with him?

MARNA (*going*). You're disgusting.

She slams the door. EDWARD *finds his Bartok score and sits down with it.*

HUGH *enters in his dressing-gown looking bleary. He makes for the scotch.*

HUGH. Still up?

EDWARD. No.

HUGH. I couldn't sleep.

EDWARD. Good.

HUGH. Can't say I liked the look of our new man at forty-eight.

EDWARD. Why?

HUGH. Looks as if he's been through it. Can't stand people who've been through it. (*He drinks.*) This scotch tastes peculiar. You haven't pissed in it have you?

EDWARD. Not after seeing you drink it by the neck once or twice. Wouldn't want to catch anything.

HUGH (*sits*). You simply can't relate to me — can you Edward?

EDWARD. I thought I was related to you. By marriage.

HUGH. Oh Christ. I give up.

EDWARD. I wish you would.

HUGH. You're so obstinately retarded in your views on women. They've flown the coop, Edward. (*Pause.*) I almost envy you being able to toddle round the world sawing away at that cello of yours. Gets you away from it, if you see what I mean. Gets you away from the . . . the strain it is. With women nowadays. (*Pause.*) The Provost of my college put it in a nutshell. 'Gentlemen', he said. 'We greet the new feminist order with aplomb. But, as it were, from behind firmly clenched teeth.'

EDWARD. You're a riveting crowd down there in Oxford. Or is it up?

Pause.

HUGH. There's something I wanted to ask you.

EDWARD. Fire away.

HUGH. If you won't take it amiss.

EDWARD. Teeth firmly clenched.

HUGH. When we're all in Oxford —

EDWARD. Yes?

HUGH. Have you and Marna ever had it off downstairs?

EDWARD. Frequently.

A pause. HUGH *drains his glass and goes to the door.*

HUGH. I'm deeply hurt Edward. (*He goes out.*)

EDWARD *finds the binoculars and goes to the window.*

Fade out.

Fade in:

Scene Three:

Lunchtime the following day. MARNA *enters with* OTTO *and starts pouring drinks.*

MARNA. How's it going over there? I've had a rotten morning.
A rotten week. The culmination, Otto — of ten years'
devotion to the cause of political prisoners from Vladivostock
to Valparaiso. I wonder if anybody realises how carefully we
check and recheck every single allegation. Every statement,
every detail. We're absolute fanatics. Then this morning. Well.
Latin America's my thing and has been for a couple of years.
I handed in a laboriously compiled draft report a couple of
days ago. Only to be informed this morning by the boss cow
that I've written the most incoherent document she's ever set
eyes on. (*Pause.*) 'Heads would roll' — said this pompous udder
whose slave I am. 'Were it not contrary to the spirit in which
we condemn those who do solve their problems that way.'

Very wry, she thinks she is. (*She drinks.*) It's so damned demoralising to give ten years of one's life to the suffering and injustice of an entire planet. I mean there's Edward fussing over his boeuf bourgignon in the kitchen — and all I can see is an endless row of people. All shapes, sizes and colours. With electrodes clipped to their genitals. (*She drinks.*) I know he cares as much as I do but he hardly lives with it. Well who can? I shouldn't think it's on your mind twenty-four hours a day — is it?

OTTO. I'm afraid not.

MARNA. Please don't look at me like that. I'm rigid with tension. I could scream.

OTTO. How am I looking?

MARNA. Oh I see you're wondering — in a superior sort of way — what I'd do with my guilt if they released them all suddenly, overnight. (*Pause.*) Why do I only have to feel passionate about something for an utterly false tone to creep into my voice? It's so humiliating.

OTTO. But I admire what you are doing. I know what it is to be unlawfully imprisoned. To disappear from the world and no one knows where you are. Beaten. Degraded. (*Pause.*) I know because the Gestapo had me for six weeks in nineteen thirty-seven. I was then sent to a camp. Some people in Berlin used their money and influence to buy me out — or I think I would not be here.

Pause.

MARNA. I'm sorry. I don't know why I hung it on you. But quite often it's as if people think there's something vaguely despicable about what I'm doing. (*Pause.*) Or the reasons why.

OTTO. There's nothing shameful, Mrs Croft. About guilt as a motivation for doing something honourable.

Pause.

MARNA. Marna. (*Pause.*) Oh dear. Oh hell. You're so incredibly sympathetic. I think I'm going to cry —

She hurries out. HUGH *enters. He looks back a moment before he closes the door. He stands looking at* OTTO *for a pause.*

HUGH. What's with Marna?

OTTO. Why don't you ask her?

HUGH. The snag about putting that question to people. Is that they tend to give pretty exhaustive answers. I'm not up to it. (*He crosses to look out with glasses*.) Doesn't look as if you've got much furniture.

OTTO. A few antiques which were my sister's. Like the house.

HUGH. It's a paradox really. She's doing her work incompetently because it's far beneath her capabilities.

OTTO. Or because she's unhappy.

HUGH. Marna unhappy? I think she's got her life organised brilliantly. (*He turns, puts down the glasses*.) Let's get it over with, shall we?

Pause.

OTTO. I thought you might wish to.

HUGH. You looked as if you could strangle me on the spot last night.

OTTO. Well, you see. I gave up the life I had so slowly and painfully made for myself in London — for Rinaldo. (*Pause*.) Did the woman you married know you are bisexual?

HUGH. Did you think you owned him?

OTTO. For one whole year I said nothing about his affair with you. He was very young — and I accepted it.

HUGH. He used to say you were suffocating him. That oh yes, you were very forebearing and all that. But you wanted to possess him like your bloody Kokoschka drawing, and the what was it? A Cezanne water colour?

OTTO. Whilst — you?

HUGH. All I wanted was to screw him.

OTTO. He thought you loved him.

HUGH. Look. I had to throw him out. Dammit I was twenty-eight. I had a double first and a doctorate. A fellowship lined up. I had Muriel fawning over me and she was loaded. We were planning to get married. (*Pause*.) As who should know better than you and I — things were different in those days. Not just the law, either.

Pause.

OTTO. Did he also tell you the Kokoschka — the Cezanne. Were smuggled out to me from Prague by my father? (*Pause*.) And what happened to my family?

HUGH. The little swine had the nerve to show up at the porter's lodge in my college one day. We had an almighty row and I knew there'd be more of them. I borrowed some money off Muriel and offered him his air fare to Canada. One way. That was the deal. (*Pause*.) So. I had him back on the train to Paddington before you could say Valpolicella.

OTTO. To me. Back to me.

HUGH. Hardly my fault if you were besotted enough to follow him to Montreal.

OTTO. And yet later you coaxed him away from me. Back to England. (*Pause*.) To Oxford? Once you were safely married?

HUGH. Is that what he told you? He was the most implausible liar I ever met. Didn't you notice?

OTTO. So in fact. You never saw him when he returned?

Pause.

HUGH. He showed up in Oxford again once. Yes. Most unflattering about the sort of life he'd been leading with you up in the frozen north. Had some very quaint snaps, too. In the Rockies, was it? Skis and woolly pom-pom hats. I could hardly believe my eyes and ears but he kept them in an Italian translation of Goethe he said you'd given him. I suppose you knew the wretched little bugger could hardly read.

Pause.

OTTO. I used to read to him.

HUGH. He was very funny about that too. Goethe? You must have been out of your mind.

OTTO. However. You threw him out once more.

HUGH. You don't spend two years with a woman like Muriel without learning something. I nearly broke his neck. Exit forever one chastened little wop from the city of dreaming spires.

Pause.

OTTO. I had two years of the greatest happiness in my life with Rinaldo. (*Pause*.) I adored him.

HUGH. A little narcissist who could hardly distinguish between passion and hysteria? (*Pause*.) It's interesting, isn't it? That psychoanalysts can balls up their lives as doggedly as anyone else.

OTTO (*as* MARNA *enters woozily with a drink*). You don't know what became of him then?

HUGH. For all I know he's back there shagging sheep in Sardinia.

MARNA. Who is? I wish Edward would. Not with sheep, of course. I just mean I wish he'd run into some nice woman who could give him an erection. (*She drinks*.) What are you two looking so morbid about? Are you starving? I must confess I'm a wee bit sloshed. (*Sitting*.) It only takes three drinks with me. (*She drinks*.) Edward — who tends to confide when cooking — has just been telling me. That the nearest he's ever got to infidelity was in Bangkok last summer. He let some pathetic British Council man have a Chinese whore on his — Edward's — American express card. (*Rising*.) Do I smell burning flesh? Or is it I'm one of those people who simply can't leave their work at the office? (*She goes out*.)

HUGH. You wouldn't believe it. I'm obsessed by her. An extraordinary woman. We're very lucky, the three of us. Get on like a house on fire.

OTTO. Perhaps it is.

HUGH. Mind you she's pretty obsessed herself.

OTTO. By what?

HUGH. Torture, mainly.

OTTO. How do people arrange these things nowadays?

HUGH. How? Well I suppose you arrest a chap. Bung him in a cellar. Strip him naked and hook him up to the electric light. I should think it's all pretty straightforward.

OTTO. I meant, of course. Three living together.

HUGH. Ah but we don't you see. Marna wouldn't wear that. She still has a vestigial sense of propriety. So we commute. I can sleep with her in Oxford but not in London. Edward vice-versa.

OTTO. You wrote love letters to Rinaldo in Montreal.

HUGH. Once or twice. Stinking drunk. (*Pause*.) Lust letters.

OTTO. You didn't love him at all?

HUGH. Really, Dottore!

OTTO. Nor your wife?

HUGH. At any rate she ended up in a looney bin. So I must have got through to her somehow.

OTTO. Do you love Marna?

HUGH. What on earth's the matter with you?

Pause.

OTTO. The matter is. That I loathe you.

Pause.

HUGH. How would you diagnose a man who — mentally speaking — fancies he's like one of those Victorian clusters of wax fruit? You know? With a glass bell thing on top. (*As* EDWARD *enters with a beer.*) Is it a classical syndrome? Wax apples. Pears. Grapes and so on. (*To* EDWARD:) With one of those greeny glass domes —

EDWARD. Who told you about that?

HUGH. Hawthorne did. At High Table the other night. It's getting him down, rather. You remember Hawthorne? You ought to. You've swigged his port often enough. He's planning a sabbatical with a particle accelerator in Switzerland. If, that is, his shrink manages to get the glass lid off before P.J. goes dare I say? Entirely wax bananas.

EDWARD. Poor old Hawthorne. (*Pause.*) Curious. I often feel a bit like that myself.

HUGH. Cut off somewhat? I'd say that's your permanent condition, Edward.

EDWARD. It isn't something you heard from Marna?

HUGH. Doesn't know Hawthorne. Might know the redoubtable Gerda. (*Pause.*) But Marna wouldn't dream of passing on a thing like that about you Edward.

EDWARD *sits. Sips his beer. Stares at* HUGH.

EDWARD. How's Muriel?

A slight pause.

HUGH (*goes, calling out*): Marna —

OTTO *and* EDWARD *regard each other impassively.* EDWARD *smiles.*

EDWARD. Wait till you taste my boeuf bourgignon.

Pause.

OTTO. As a friend. I confess I'm puzzled by what you seem to be enduring here Edward. (*Pause.*) You couldn't go on with a new analyst but — you married Marna? Would it have been around that time?

EDWARD. It's beginning to feel like one of our old sessions. What about you though? You packed it in from the other side.

OTTO. I will be honest. (*Pause.*) I came to the conclusion one day . . . I had not the stamina to go on. I imply no disillusion with the work. (*Pause.*) But I thought I myself had become unfit. I am more interested just now in you and your wife though.

Pause.

EDWARD. Right at the beginning I nursed her through a very destructive affair. With one of those revolutionaries who seem to care about humanity in general — but not actual individual people. (*Pause.*) One day when we were spending a weekend by the sea she tried to commit suicide. Tried to drown herself. (*Pause.*) Well I saw her through that as well. She was awfully vulnerable. And she really seemed to turn to me from then on. (*Pause.*) Came to love me, I'd say. Yes and I her, even more. (*Pause.*) She's brave and good when you know her. She cares. (*Pause.*) You may not think so—

Pause. OTTO *crosses to the window.*

OTTO (*as* HUGH *enters*). I didn't come back to live in that house. I shall be off soon.

EDWARD. So why bother to move in?

OTTO. I intend to rent it. There's a lot to be done first.

HUGH (*to* EDWARD): You're needed in the kitchen.

EDWARD. Why?

HUGH. Seems I've reduced her to tears.

EDWARD. Why?

HUGH. Mental condition of my wife strictly off limits, old son.

Not a theme for conjugal gossip.

EDWARD. I thought you didn't believe in them.

HUGH. What?

EDWARD. Limits.

HUGH. It must be something you bring out in me Edward. Like hives, or psychosomatic asthma. I wish you'd do something about her. It's not my style at all to cut a woman down and than waste time chatting her up again.

EDWARD *goes*.

OTTO. It is true your wife is mentally ill?

HUGH. Bull's eye first time, Dottore. You must have been a top man in yours. Ex-wife, should've said. (*Pause*.) Glad to know you're moving on. I was beginning to think you were intent on making trouble. What? After nearly twenty years? There are limits, after all. It really has been a trying week. Take Tuesday. I lose some brilliant bugger's thesis in a taxi. She spends a macabre afternoon boning up on sensory deprivation. We get back here. Slump down with a couple of camparis. And he totters in from Amsterdam — trailing dogshit all over the floor as usual — to inform us KLM's flown his cello to Karachi. (*Pause*.) He was murderous. So naturally we talk him through it and talk him through it for hours. One in the morning, Marna catches him with a hammer skulking off to smash KLM's windows in New Bond Street. No more talk, says Edward. Either we give him his valium back or it's goodbye KLM. Needless to say we flushed his valium down the drain when we first started this having it all out in the open therapy. I thought he was going to kill us both. Then the phone rings. KLM. His bloody cello's on its way from Heathrow. Too late for me. By now I'm homicidal and verbalising all this excitement like mad. Marna was still talking me through that one at breakfast time. I mean do you wonder if the fate of some Italian slut like Rinaldo leaves me unmoved in the circumstances?

Pause.

OTTO. I found out that he did go back to Italy. To Rome. Where he and some old queen took an overdose together one night. (*Pause*.) Which is the more tragic because I would willingly have taken him back. On any terms.

HUGH. Christ you and Edward should hit it off nicely. Two peas in a pod. Take him back to Goethe and Mahler? Mozart and Hauptmann? Ski-ing weekends up there in the pines with a bunch of ageing screwed-up psychoanalysts? When he wasn't laughing he absolutely hated it.

OTTO *slowly crosses to the window. He looks out.*

OTTO. I had never intended to stay in that house. I am getting old. I had thought to die in the sun somewhere. (*Pause.*) I came there late one night when it was first empty. I wanted to be quiet for an hour in the house where Frieda and I had known a little peace together long ago. (*Pause.*) Do we not all yearn for childhood sometimes? And of course all from her childhood and mine has long been obliterated. (*Pause.*) I looked across the street. This lamp here was on. The curtains drawn back. Marna stood naked. You were kneeling in front of her. (*Pause.*) I recognised you then. The lamplight caught your face —

HUGH. I'm not allowed actual intercourse you know, in this temple of frustration.

OTTO. Rinaldo had snapshots of you too. More appropriately in your case — next to the money in his wallet.

HUGH. You were the rich one by his standards. He didn't get much out of me I can tell you. D'you think he'd have lived with me when he could shack up with you in Canada? No. He'd have thought that very whimsical. And Rinaldo's chief aim in life was to end up not with a whim but a banker.

Pause.

OTTO. Edward was standing in the doorway that night when I looked.

HUGH. He is a bit freaky isn't he? Must be plain as a pikestaff to a professional.

OTTO *turns slowly from the window. He and* HUGH *look at each other.* MARNA *appears at the door.*

MARNA. Lunch is ready —

OTTO *takes a gun and fires at* HUGH. MARNA *screams.*

Blackout.

Act Two

Scene One:

Afternoon the same day. Fade up slowly on EDWARD. He stands at the window looking out. He turns, slowly. He is wearing the Nigerian mask. He takes it off. He looks out.

MARNA enters. She sits.

A pause.

MARNA. Where do we go from here then?

EDWARD. How is he?

MARNA. Shocked. Speechless. Emitting the occasional whimper.

EDWARD. Yes. I thought he'd lay it on a bit.

MARNA. Edward. He's had the lobe of one ear shot away.

EDWARD. Nicked.

MARNA. There was a lot of blood, anyway.

EDWARD. Good thing we had a doctor in the house.

MARNA. Don't. Please. I feel awful. I'm still trembling.

EDWARD. Otto seems pretty shaken, too.

MARNA. The man's a maniac. It was no accident. He deliberately shot Hugh. That bullet could have gone through his head. And why was he carrying a gun in the first place? I couldn't believe it. And now it seems even more unreal. (*Pause.*) Have you been over there? Have you tried to have it out with him?

EDWARD. I did pop over to see how he's getting on.

MARNA. How he's getting on!

EDWARD. How are you getting on?

MARNA. I'm absolutely bloody appalled.

EDWARD. Maybe he's a marksman. Maybe he has a row of silver cups. Been years in a gun-toting society.

MARNA. He had nothing to say for himself? No explanation.

EDWARD. No. (*Pause*.) Looked a bit glazed though.

MARNA. Well I'm furious. I think we ought to do something.

EDWARD. Report it?

MARNA. Shouldn't we?

EDWARD. No real harm done.

Pause.

MARNA You're enjoying it, aren't you? My God you're cockahoop.

Pause.

EDWARD. I am, rather.

MARNA. I wonder how you'd feel if he'd killed him.

EDWARD. I've often daydreamed about liquidating our man in Oxford myself.

MARNA. I don't think I'm getting through to you.

EDWARD. Oh you are. You always do. One way or another.

MARNA. Aren't you curious?

EDWARD. Absolutely on tenterhooks.

MARNA. Why should you be stonewalling? Do you know something I don't?

EDWARD. I suspect what it is with old Otto. He spent half a lifetime talking things through with people. Then he walks in here. Claps eyes on Hugh. Listens to him braying on. And realises it's been a vocation wasted.

MARNA. What has?

EDWARD. He used to be a psychoanalyst.

Pause.

MARNA. Is that how you came to know him? Professionally?

EDWARD. It sticks out a mile with Hugh if you ask me. Kindest thing you could do is put him out of his misery. Or ours.

MARNA. I want to know, Edward.

Pause.

EDWARD. Five days a week for a few months. Then he went to Canada. Packed it in, over there. Saw the light. Saw right through psychoanalysis and came out on the other side. Years and years ago.

Pause.

MARNA. Why did you go to him?

EDWARD. You know how it is. I woke up one morning panic-stricken. (*Pause.*) Palpitations. Sweating. Shaking from head to foot. Had a physical examination. Nothing wrong. Fit as a fiddle. (*Pause.*) But it didn't go away.

MARNA. Why did you never tell me?

EDWARD. Have you forgotten? You weren't very interested in me for a long time. Then it was too late.

Pause.

MARNA. But it went away?

EDWARD. When I started playing with Hans and Polly Koenig. (*Pause.*) Remember Polly?

MARNA. How do we know he didn't intend to kill Hugh?

EDWARD. Shouldn't think so.

MARNA. But if he did?

EDWARD. I think he was just playing it by ear.

MARNA (*rising*). You can't resist — can you? I'll leave you to gloat.

EDWARD. You don't want to talk about it?

MARNA. No.

EDWARD. That's a daring innovation.

MARNA *starts to go out then turns back.* HUGH *enters quietly behind her. He has a bandage round his head with a fat gauze dressing over the right ear.*

MARNA. I want to know why.

EDWARD. Why what?

MARNA. And please don't start that again. I want to know why Otto Neumann should wish to harm somebody he's only just met.

HUGH. No mystery there at all. Sexual envy. And coming from a psychoanalyst I must say I find it rather bizarre. I trust I can rely on you both as witnesses? Yes, Edward. I meant you especially of course. Because I intend to have the sod behind bars. Or. If I can dredge up a little charity. Bunged into some suitable institution.

Pause.

MARNA. Sexual envy?

HUGH. Right. And the incredible thing is. It's been festering in the little swine for about fifteen years. Can you believe it? My God there's nothing live and let live about these mind doctors — is there? (*He gets a drink.*)

MARNA. What's been festering?

HUGH. I shall have to lie down. (*He sprawls on the couch.*) I feel as if I've been cuffed on the head by a bloody rhino. God what an experience. Who does he think he is? Uncle Vanya?

Pause.

MARNA. Hugh —

HUGH. Yes darling.

MARNA. Tell please.

HUGH. Before you start putting me on trial. May I remind you I'm the victim of a recent homicidal attack? That I'm amazed — if not entirely grateful — to be alive? (*Pause.*) I mean if you're going to be shrill, Marna. You've got competition. There's a ringing in my skull like somebody twanging a high tension cable.

MARNA. I've no intention of trying to put you on trial.

HUGH. That's the spirit. (*Pause: to* EDWARD:) What are you grinning at?

EDWARD. Sorry. It's the bandage.

HUGH. What about it? Not that there wasn't something pretty macabre about being trussed up by your own murderer.

EDWARD Makes you look a bit raffish, that's all.

HUGH. Quite. And my brains would've looked quite raffish too, wouldn't they? Splattered all over your wall. (*Pause: to*

MARNA:) Might as well let you have it straight between the eyes. Fact is. Otto and I once shared a lover and it seems not only did I ruin his life but he still can't forgive me. What stamina for vengeance the man must have.

Pause.

MARNA. Who was she?

HUGH. Wasn't a she it was a he.

Pause.

MARNA. You — and a man?

HUGH. What's so bloody baffling about that? My father was queer. My grandfather was queer. And his father before him.

Pause.

MARNA. I see.

HUGH. I knew you'd take it on the chin.

MARNA. Runs in the family. That it?

HUGH. Dynastic. Grandpa used to say it was the sort of thing that kept the Tories in touch with the working classes. (*To* EDWARD:) I'll bet you're tickled pink. Very much the kind of thing to have you in fits — eh? Like having her behind my back. Or should I say under my roof? In Oxford. Frequently.

MARNA. If he told you that he was lying.

HUGH. Come on.

MARNA. What about you? D'you mean to say you can shuttle about between men and women just like that?

HUGH. It's a knack bisexuals have you know.

MARNA. You actually had a physical relationship with this whoever he was?

HUGH. Shall we say — less than spiritual but more than platonic. Must we pursue it just now? I mean haven't you got your priorities a bit screwed up Marna? We've got a homicidal shrink across the road. Haven't the awful implications of that struck home? The blow to the hopes and aspirations of an entire species? (*Pause.*) D'you really want to sit about chewing the fat re my sex life in the year dot?

MARNA. No. Your sex life now.

HUGH. In front of that grinning cellist? Look at him. Hawthorne had your number all right: intriguing chap but an objective shit.

EDWARD. Wouldn't dream of discussing it behind your back though, Hugh.

HUGH. I refuse to discuss it at all.

MARNA. Very well. But in that case I don't see how we can go on.

EDWARD. Good. Let's throw him out.

HUGH. After what I've put into your marriage? Do you think she'd still be here if it weren't for me?

EDWARD. I was thinking of throwing you both out as a matter of fact.

Pause.

MARNA (*to* EDWARD): You were what?

Pause.

EDWARD. It was Polly Koenig's firm conviction. That you only agreed to marry me when you found out how much she loved me. (*To* HUGH:) She came round here one afternoon when Polly and I were rolling about on the bare boards with a bottle of champagne. Simon and Garfunkeling like crazy we were. You ever been Garfunkeled? It defies description. I mean you see. There was the awkward problem that I liked Polly a lot more than Marna (*Pause.*) Loved Marna but didn't like her all that much. Plus which, making love with Polly was sheer music. It gave me the same feeling I had when we played the Schubert E flat. (*To* MARNA:) Whereas you tended to make me feel you were dispensing charity. Not to mention the public hints about my sexual inadequacy. The comparisons with a pantheon of previous lovers. In among which that revolutionary shag Schwartzers was merely the latest and greatest. (*To* HUGH:) Yes. It's just come back to me. The evening of that day with Polly, it was Marna who suggested Southwold. A summer's evening. Windows open. Flower-scented breezes. Walls drenched with Polly's Dom Perignon. (*Pause.*) I think that summer was the most lovely and poignant in all my life. She and Hans and I played in Karlsruhe. In Perugia and Avignon. In Trieste and Dubrovnik. We were inspired. We won standing ovations. Dammit all when I look back on it, Polly was magic.

The very air glowed around her. (*Pause*.) And I — (*To* MARNA:) I married you for love? (*Pause*.) Yes you stood there almost where you are now. And what had you decided? To cut your losses with me? Or just that together we'd break Polly's heart? (*Pause*.) Which we did. And Hans said that was the end of the trio. Which it was. (*Pause*.) You can get rattled because one of his old flames was a man? (*The doorbell rings*.) Is that the measure of your capacity for outrage nowadays?

The doorbell rings again.

MARNA. If that's Otto Neumann.

EDWARD *slaps her face hard.*

EDWARD. Enough! (*He goes out*.)

MARNA *stands touching her cheek. A long silence. She crosses to* HUGH. *She stands looking down at him.*

MARNA. Did you bugger him?

HUGH. What?

MARNA. Did you do that as well? Have you always had men too? (*Pause*.) Since me?

Pause.

HUGH. I loved him.

MARNA. Yes? (*Pause*.) So you married Muriel?

Pause.

HUGH. I've been proud of that love. And ashamed of that marriage. All my life since. (*Pause*.) I think Rinaldo must have been my Polly. (*Pause*.) How did Edward put it? Yes. The very air glowed around him. (*Pause*.) It was like that.

MARNA *crosses to the door: turns.*

MARNA. He was using her. Oh yes he was. Even if he couldn't and can't admit it. (*Pause*.) He'd been hanging round me for years. Quietly. Shyly. Always there. Always available in a crisis. Indefatigably gentle. Remorselessly kind. (*Pause*.) I was told she was wild about him. Besotted. It's true the three of them played brilliantly together. I've never known Edward like he was then. He was manic. He glittered. (*Pause*.) I was exhausted that summer. Worn out. Because Jean-Jacques. The running family gag in this house. Was my first and only true love. (*Pause*.) So there we are. Tit for tat. After Jean-Jacques I thought it didn't matter who had me. So why not give in to Edward? Make some kind of life. (*Pause.*) I've only been able to trust you because I thought you were heartless. (*She goes out.*)

HUGH *gets up to refill his glass and goes back to lie on the couch.*

OTTO *enters. He stands just inside the door.*

OTTO. May I come in?

HUGH. Made a real hash of it didn't you?

Pause.

OTTO. May I sit down?

HUGH. May I may I. What's the matter with you? Yes. Do. Sit down for Christ's sake.

OTTO *takes a straightbacked chair to the couch.*

HUGH. You look as if you need a drink. Have a big one. It's my whisky. (*As* OTTO *gets himself a drink.*) My whisky under his roof. His whisky under mine. We don't like to get into a rut.

OTTO. I thought that if you could bear it. I might perhaps change the dressing.

HUGH. Well I couldn't bear it. It's as well I passed out when you shot me or I'd have screamed if you came anywhere near.

OTTO (*sits*). It is very painful still?

HUGH. Of course it bloody is. You saw it. Looks as if it's been chewed by a pterodactyl. Needless to say. Edward takes the lighter view that the bandage makes me look a bit comical. She on the other hand seems more preoccupied with the question of whether Rinaldo and I were actual sodomites.

OTTO. So you told them. (*Pause.*) I am glad.

HUGH. Can you imagine? He's mad at her because she's mad at me because I once had a male lover. (*He drinks.*) They've no idea, have they? (*Pause: he touches the bandage.*) Does it look raffish? I'm not totally averse to looking raffish.

OTTO. I'm sure Edward's frivolity springs only from relief.

HUGH. That you didn't finish me off? More like he's trying to hide his disappointment. I know it's your field and all that, but I prefer Bainbridge's Law: the most vicious one. (*Pause.*)

I took a peek in the mirror before I came down. Well, I thought. If not quite comical — certainly unheroic. Might go better with a cutlass and a plumed hat, eh? (*Pause.*) Did you intend to kill me?

Pause.

OTTO. I don't know.

HUGH. Left that little decision to our unconscious did we? But we did bring the gun along though. Seems to me your bloody unconscious had something nasty in mind. No? What's the latest dogma on them Dottore? Because I haven't got one.

OTTO. I'm an excellent shot.

HUGH. That's a fine bit of post hoc reassurance.

OTTO. Perhaps my unconscious wished only to administer a severe shock.

HUGH. How can you talk about it as if you weren't actually present when the gun went off?

Pause.

OTTO. Well. Of course. One takes the responsibility for it.

HUGH. I should bloody well hope so.

Pause.

OTTO. An impulse.

HUGH. You should try my method. I've got most of Edward's impulses ironed out in six months flat.

Pause.

OTTO. Rinaldo —

HUGH. My God what a long time to bear a grudge. What's the matter with you?

Pause.

OTTO. When I pulled the trigger. It was as if years of bitterness and isolation exploded in me.

HUGH. I've no objection to that part of it. But they very nearly exploded in my skull. You can't hold me responsible.

Pause.

OTTO. No.

Pause.

HUGH. You went to Italy looking for him?

OTTO. That is how I found out.

Pause.

HUGH. So the stupid little sod finally goes to bed in Rome with an old queen and a bottle of pills.

OTTO. Yes.

Pause.

HUGH. Never did know where to draw the line, did he?

Pause.

OTTO. He believed he could do anything to me and survive the consequences. Perhaps he thought he could do the same to himself. He did everything recklessly. I think the idea of his own death was quite unreal to him.

HUGH. I always thought it didn't matter what I did to him. (*Pause.*) I thought him utterly shallow. (*Pause.*) Beautiful. Light. Funny. Gay in the true sense. (*Pause.*) And frighteningly superficial.

HUGH *is stretched out full length on the couch.* OTTO *goes to sit beside him.*

OTTO. That would make him less of an obstacle to whatever else you wanted. If there was nothing to him — perhaps you could behave as if there were no one there? (*He smiles gently.*) As I might have said if I were sitting behind the couch instead of on it.

Pause.

HUGH. Once I'd turned my back on him. Once I'd married Muriel —

Pause.

OTTO. Yes?

HUGH. From then on —

Pause.

OTTO. Yes?

Pause.

HUGH. Before Canada. He commuted between us. Didn't he?

OTTO. He did.

Pause.

HUGH. Before Muriel. I used to have a fantasy that I'd cut him out. (*Pause.*) Make you love me. (*Pause.*) Steal you.

Pause.

OTTO. Yes. A fantasy.

HUGH. Otto —

OTTO. I listen.

Pause.

HUGH. Hold me —

OTTO *takes him in his arms.*

Fade out.

Fade in:

Scene Two:

Late evening the same day. MARNA *stands looking across the street through the binoculars.*

EDWARD *enters wearing a light top coat. He takes it off and sits. A long pause.*

EDWARD. How did the recording go, Edward?

MARNA (*puts the glasses down, sits*). All right. So how did it go?

EDWARD. I played all the right notes, anyway. (*Pause.*) I was fiendishly good as a matter of fact.

Long pause.

MARNA. They've been across the street together. Ever since you went out.

EDWARD. And you've been watching.

MARNA. On and off.

Long pause.

EDWARD. See anything?

MARNA. No.

Pause.

EDWARD. I'm very tired.

MARNA. You didn't tell me you were recording.

EDWARD. In the circumstances I didn't think you'd hear me.

MARNA. So why make a thing of it when you come in?

Pause.

EDWARD. You look pale. (*Pause.*) Drawn.

MARNA. Old, you mean.

EDWARD. No. (*Pause.*) Hardly older than when we first met.

MARNA. Come come.

EDWARD. Really.

Pause.

MARNA. Before Polly. Before Jean-Jacques.

EDWARD. Before everybody, when you come to think of it.

MARNA. Yes I didn't seem to go in for friends. (*Pause.*) People in college used to say who is he? Is he political? A what? A cellist? Jesus Christ. How did you meet him? (*Pause.*) We were arrested together, I'd say. (*Pause.*) He fell in love with me on a demonstration. Yes. He is a bit of a bore.

Pause.

EDWARD. You gave me a quick rundown on socialist theory in the black maria.

MARNA. Not your thing at all, was it?

EDWARD. I shared my toffees with you.

MARNA. Oh, Edward.

EDWARD. It was awful when they split us up at the police station.

MARNA. You were so nervous. Such a rabbit.

EDWARD. Shit scared.

MARNA. Well. It all came to nothing.

EDWARD. I was in a cell with eight blokes who sang 'We shall overcome' half the night. Yes. I will say. Hardly any overcoming took place at all. (*Pause*.) I lost a score of the Dvořák F minor somewhere in the cop shop.

Pause.

MARNA. Did you ever suspect he's bisexual?

EDWARD. I do feel as if I've known you all my life.

MARNA. I thought a man might sense it.

EDWARD. I never caught on with Otto either. I think I'd have burst into tears if somebody'd told me my analyst was queer.

MARNA. Gay.

EDWARD. They hadn't expropriated the word in those days.

Pause.

MARNA. Of course. It doesn't make any difference to one's feelings.

EDWARD. Course not. Not in these days.

Pause.

MARNA. It's — my body.

EDWARD. What?

MARNA. It's his having had my body that repels me.

EDWARD. That's what always repelled me too.

MARNA. You know what I mean Edward.

EDWARD. Something anatomical.

MARNA. Exactly.

EDWARD. Can't quite take it in your stride eh?

MARNA. It's nauseating.

Pause.

EDWARD. Did you know Jean-Jacques had Polly?

MARNA. I don't believe it.

EDWARD. It's true.

MARNA. They didn't know each other.

EDWARD. She and Hans had a party here. The weekend you and

I went to Southwold. (*Pause*.) The weekend we broke her heart.

MARNA. Broke her heart!

EDWARD. It did sound better in German I agree.

MARNA. And he just happened along?

EDWARD. On his way to Venezuela.

MARNA. Peru.

EDWARD. She invited him. Polly knew people who knew everybody.

MARNA. I don't believe it.

EDWARD. I'd told her all about you and him. How he couldn't take you on because he had to spend his life jumping from one barricade to the next. (*Pause*.) Definitely on your side, Polly was. Love first, come rain or shine. That was her position.

MARNA. You discussed my private life with Polly?

EDWARD. With all and sundry. But mainly because you didn't care in those days.

Pause.

MARNA. You mean — she had him because she knew I was getting you?

EDWARD. According to Hans it wasn't quite like that. It's true once she realised Southwold was in the bag she went up the wall. But Hans didn't say Polly had Jean-Jacques. He pointed out in his somewhat teutonic fashion — it was more Jean-Jacques had Polly. He emphasised the crucial difference. (*Pause*.) Then he thrashed me.

MARNA. He what?

EDWARD. Knocked the living daylights out of me. After a concert at the Wigmore. Bashed my right ear to pulp very nearly. Which makes you wonder if there isn't a Divine Pattern after all.

MARNA. Shouldn't he rather have beaten up Jean-Jacques?

EDWARD. Hans? He wouldn't soil his knuckles on a revolutionary.

MARNA. Oh Christ, Edward.

EDWARD. Yes. I don't think Hans could have put it better himself. In any language.

A pause. MARNA crosses to the window. She finds the binoculars. She looks out.

EDWARD (*shouts*): Put the bloody things down!

She puts them down. She crosses to him.

MARNA. I shall never forgive you for hitting me today.

EDWARD. Am I losing my grip — or finding it?

Pause.

MARNA (*sits*). Shall we get a divorce now?

Pause.

EDWARD. He more or less raped Polly. You know how it is sometimes at a party. Hans didn't know whether she was drunk. Collusive. Violated. Or all three. (*Pause.*) But Jean-Jacques knew what he was doing.

MARNA. We're going to talk, Edward. About us.

EDWARD. Whereas to you he wrote sonnets. Didn't he? In Walloon, was it?

HUGH enters carrying a small hammer.

HUGH. Excuse me —

He goes to the window. He finds the binoculars. He smashes the lenses.

HUGH. There. That's better. Sorry to intrude. I'll just go up and pack.

MARNA. When you've swept up the pieces.

HUGH. I thought you regarded that as being his province.

EDWARD. You really can see why somebody'd shoot him can't you?

HUGH. She's all yours Edward.

EDWARD. You can't just chuck my wife round like a parcel.

HUGH. You've been holding out long enough. Why not try for a catch?

EDWARD. Stepping out of the rubble are you?

HUGH. Leaving the country.

EDWARD. I wish you'd tell him Marna.

MARNA. Tell him what? I've nothing to say to him.

Pause.

EDWARD. She's extremely shocked, you see. Shows no sign of recuperation. Putting up a stoic facade, that's all. It'll be a long convalescence. (*Pause.*) Have a drink.

MARNA. He can get out.

EDWARD. Have a large whisky. At least it's your own whisky.

HUGH. Did you know she thinks you're an emotional cripple?

EDWARD. Did you know I think I'm an emotional cripple?

HUGH. Stuck out a mile right from beginning, Edward. Have you tried psychoanalysis?

MARNA. Stop it!

HUGH. I hear they've gone off it altogether in New York. Deserting their analysts in droves. What's the betting skid row's chock-a-block with destitute shrinks? Mind you. I wouldn't take you on. God no. No. I wouldn't say it's hopeless. But I think you represent a case for the chemical approach. Eh? What about it?

MARNA. Stop it!

HUGH. What on earth's the matter with her?

EDWARD. Going anywhere in particular?

HUGH. Italy, we thought.

MARNA. We?

HUGH. Otto and I.

EDWARD. Love at first sight, was it?

HUGH. He wants to die in the sun.

EDWARD. They'll miss you at Balliol.

HUGH. I expect they would if I was at Balliol.

EDWARD. Is Otto dying more than most people are? I mean has he got something terminal?

HUGH. I don't think so. No. No he's as fit as a fiddle. Like a man possessed, in fact.

EDWARD. Possessed by what?

HUGH. Positively humming with energy. Head full of plans. If you ask me, he's a new man since he blew my ear off. (*Pause*.) So am I. You ought to try shooting her, Edward.

MARNA. I wish he'd put that bullet between your eyes.

HUGH. There's your cue, old man.

EDWARD. What?

HUGH. Get her on the rebound.

EDWARD. Get her?

HUGH. Sweep her off her feet. Pop the question. Put the banns up. Hire a marquee and a good caterer. I know a firm in Chelsea. Oh, I know you're going to say you're married already. But are you? Has it really been a marriage? Have you cherished each other? I mean, you can see she's gone off me. Right off. She can't get over the idea that I might have had anal intercourse with a male — consenting or otherwise. Can't you see your wife's definitely stayed the course? Still the same wholesome girl she was when they picked you up together on that demonstration. Anti-apartheid was it? Nuclear weapons? Women's rights — or was that after her time?

Pause.

MARNA (*to* EDWARD): He's knelt there. Right there. In front of me. On the very spot you're so fond of enshrining to bloody Polly. Trembling. And panting. Abject to lust. (*Pause*.) And cursed you. (*Pause*.) Whilst I stood dumb with horror. Awestruck by the irrelevance of the pair of you. Helpless. Amazed. (*Pause*.) More than once. And I've pushed him out. Reeled round this room at three and four in the morning beating the walls with my fists. Naked. Grieving. Wishing I were a hardened drinker and could just blot myself out. Pleading to some nameless power — please to let me not exist. (*Pause*.) Worst of all was when I realised I couldn't even slam the door at his back. I found myself closing it ever so gently. And why? So's not to waken you. How could either of you know about that particular reflex? Deference. Automatic. Almost instinctive. To protect the male. To yield him priority at all times. To assign him a kind of natural predominance in the order of things. (*Pause*.) This daily humiliation that offends my intelligence and leaves me weak with self-disgust.

(*More loudly*:) I've known it all my life. (*Pause*.) I'm bright.
Informed. Educated. Free. I have a husband, a lover and a job.
I know all your tricks. Your devices. Your double-think. My
God, what a lengthy uphill struggle it's been. To disinter a
woman from that incoherent fool of nineteen you met on the
demonstration. (*Pause*.) Only to find. Half-way to death. That
the small girl who'd subdue her own hysteria rather than
inconvenience my mother's husband. Is still there. (*Pause*.)
And so powerful. So dutiful. So quick off the mark. Your
slave, gentlemen. Your creature. Who's already in action
before I've even begun to think. (*Pause*.) Can't slam a door?
Have a fit? Run away? (*Pause*.) Have I really got a damned
little saboteur within who aborts the conscious grown woman?
(*Pause*.) You bet I have. (*Going to the door*:) And I hate and
despise her. (*Pause*.) This thing I was before I invented me. At
such cost. With so much pain. Self-doubt. Confusion. (*Pause*.)
But enough guts, surely. To merit being spared your contempt.

She goes out. EDWARD *and* HUGH *stand looking at each
other for a long moment.*

The outer door slams.

Pause.

EDWARD. Shall I help you pack?

HUGH. I think I'll have that drink, you know.

EDWARD. So will I. (*He gets the drinks.* HUGH *sits*.)

HUGH. You can't imagine what a relief it'll be to shack up with a
man.

EDWARD. Really?

HUGH. Can't stand oratorios.

EDWARD. What?

HUGH. I mean there she was. Sounding off about all that mind-
boggling, daunting business of being her. (*Pause*.) And I felt
the inside of my head congealing. You know? Like a dish of
brawn put out on the sill to cool. (*Pause*.) Used to be very fond
of brawn. Haven't even clapped eyes on the stuff for decades.
(*Pause*.) You spotted any brawn anywhere lately?

EDWARD *brings the drinks.*

EDWARD. Five minutes for the drink. Ten to pack.

HUGH. What?

EDWARD. Before I do an injury to the other ear.

HUGH. Now wait a minute. Just you hang on a minute Edward.

EDWARD. How dare you embark on an erotic adventure with my psychoanalyst?

HUGH. Bless you old son.

EDWARD. What?

HUGH. For a minute I thought you were going to come on strong. (*He drinks*.) Thought you were getting a touch heavy.

EDWARD (*sprawls in a chair*). Want to keep it light? (*He sips*.)

HUGH. Christ yes.

EDWARD. Just pack up and blow?

HUGH. Christ yes.

EDWARD. With the electric shaver she gave you for Christmas? And the silk dressing-gown I gave you for your birthday?

HUGH. Spoils of war, don't y'know.

Pause.

EDWARD. Do you really mean to say Otto's taking you on?

HUGH. Yes he is, as a matter of fact.

Pause.

EDWARD. It's heroic.

HUGH. Quite.

EDWARD. Not taking you on — professionally, though.

HUGH. No. Not professionally. (*Pause*.) No no no.

Pause.

EDWARD. Sexually?

HUGH. All in good time, I should think.

Pause.

EDWARD. The one-eared lover.

HUGH. Now see here, Edward —

EDWARD. Who do you think you are? Van Gogh?

Pause.

HUGH. Let's not ignore the fact. That you've been entirely complicit in the whole thing between Marna and me.

EDWARD. Side-splitting.

HUGH. What?

EDWARD. To imagine you and him in bed together.

HUGH. Cut it out will you?

EDWARD. Fondling each other.

HUGH. I'm warning you —

EDWARD. Kissing each other.

Pause.

HUGH. For your sake, Edward. I'm exerting a great deal of self-control.

EDWARD. Van Gogh now. (*Pause.*) There was a suffering creature. A tormented soul. (*Pause.*) So I understand.

HUGH. I'll be on my way.

EDWARD. What a draughtsman though. What an innovator. I mean — he did more. With only one ear on his head. Than you'd ever achieve if you had no ears at all.

HUGH (*rising*). If it'll make you happy. I concede straight away that I lack anything approaching the moral stature. Of the famous post-impressionist. (*Pause.*) Okay?

Pause.

EDWARD. I'm afraid you don't get off so easily, old Bainbridge old feller.

HUGH. Why not?

EDWARD. I wonder if Otto knows what he's getting. I suppose he ought to. He's a trained man. He knows a thing or two about the twists and turns of the human soul. Eh? Knows the human psyche like the back of his hand.

HUGH. Shouldn't you be thinking more about where you stand with your wife?

EDWARD. We're inseparable.

Pause.

HUGH. It's been an appalling experience with you two.

EDWARD. It hasn't been much fun with you either.

Pause.

HUGH. We got on rather well though. You and I.

EDWARD. Superficially.

Pause.

HUGH. Quite good sparring partners. In a way.

EDWARD. We got through it.

HUGH. With an astonishing lack of rancour. When you come to think about it.

EDWARD. I couldn't bear to think about it.

Pause.

HUGH. Objectively. (*Pause.*) Objectively I'd say she felt less cornered. (*Pause.*) With the two of us.

Pause.

EDWARD. Piss off.

Pause.

HUGH. He wants to see you.

EDWARD. Tell him to pop over.

HUGH. It's quite late.

Pause.

EDWARD. She'll stay out walking. Till one or two in the morning. (*Pause.*) That's what she used to do before you moved in. (*Pause.*) I shall wait up for her.

HUGH *rises. He crosses to the window.*

HUGH. She's standing under the streetlamp at the corner.

Pause.

EDWARD. There was a time when she used to accost people. (*Pause.*) Till one night a bloke took her up on it.

Pause.

HUGH. She bolted?

EDWARD. He did. Because Marna stood there in the street

screaming.

HUGH. For dear life, eh?

Pause.

EDWARD. For me. (*Pause.*) Stood there shouting my name.

Pause.

HUGH. She's gone now. (*Turning:*) Tell you what. I'll tell him he can come over. Just throw my stuff into a case and give it to him will you?

EDWARD. All right.

HUGH. I'll be off then. (*He puts his hand out.*) Goodbye Edward.

They shake hands.

At the door, HUGH *turns.*

HUGH. What don't I get off so easily? (*Pause.*) Just what exactly? What did you mean?

Pause.

EDWARD. You might have to love him. (*Pause.*) There might be no alternative this time. (*Pause.*) Not this late in the day.

Pause.

HUGH. End up trundling his wheelchair down the Adriatic coast?

EDWARD. That sort of thing.

Pause.

HUGH. I hope he lives for ever. But when he does go. I'd like to help him to die gently.

EDWARD. In the sun — eh?

HUGH. That's right.

EDWARD. On a nice warm terrace. Couple of lizards basking on the stones. (*Pause.*) Bottle of chilled wine. (*Pause.*) A spot of Mahler?

HUGH. Ugh.

EDWARD. Second and Third symphonies his favourites. As I recall.

Pause.

HUGH. At least I can read to him in German. He might like that.

EDWARD. Try Goethe. He's mad about Goethe.

Pause.

HUGH. Ciao, Edward.

HUGH *goes.*

Fade out.

Fade in:

Scene Three:

Later. EDWARD is asleep by the window. A pigskin suitcase in the centre. MARNA and OTTO enter quietly. MARNA stands over EDWARD.

MARNA. He won't be easy to wake up. He has this knack in a crisis. Of falling into a kind of self-induced coma.

Pause.

OTTO. I'll come back tomorrow.

MARNA. No. Sit down. Have a drink.

OTTO. So late?

Pause.

MARNA. When this happens I usually sit by him till he wakes up. What'll you have?

OTTO. A scotch and water if I may.

She gets the drink. OTTO sits on the couch looking at EDWARD.

OTTO. Hugh asked me to take his case.

MARNA. That's it over there. (*Pause.*) Pigskin. We bought it in Florence together last year. (*Pause.*) What are you up to?

OTTO. I had come to make amends, if possible. To say goodbye. (*Pause.*) I think I must have rung the bell twice. Then I saw you coming up the street.

MARNA (*bringing the drink*). What are you up to with him, I meant. (*She points at the window.*) With that one.

Pause.

OTTO. Hugh broke down. (*Pause.*) He said: 'hold me'. (*Pause.*) I put my arms round him. (*Pause.*) Then I took him away.

MARNA. I find it all somewhat bizarre. (*Pause.*) I resent that. (*She drinks.*) You make me feel my standards of bizarrerie must be quite provincial. (*She points two fingers at him.*) Bang bang!

Pause.

OTTO. This encounter has been painful for me too Mrs Croft.

MARNA. I'd hardly call it an encounter. Seems more like a rout if you ask me. (*Pause.*) You could have walked away from us. (*Pause.*) We'd found a way to live. (*She drinks.*) I think you must be quite a ruthless person. (*She crosses to look down at EDWARD.*) Most men age well don't they? He was twenty-three when I first met him and . . . and so fine looking. (*Pause.*) D'you know he's never played for me? Not in private. Never at home. (*Pause.*) He's often said he was playing for me when I was at one of his concerts. Amsterdam was the first time I actually saw him play. (*Pause.*) I thought: 'Why this is somebody else entirely. Almost physically different. Such authority. Such tremendous power. Can that be Edward?' (*Pause.*) And of course in a way it isn't. (*Pause.*) He thinks that himself. (*Pause.*) Twenty years ago I thought people with extraordinary gifts . . . must surely be extraordinary people too. But Edward says its completely impersonal. He says he doesn't feel he personally can take any credit for his music whatsoever.

EDWARD *yawns and stretches, his eyes still closed.*

EDWARD. I didn't put it quite like that. (*Pause.*) Isn't it peaceful without Hugh? (*Pause: he opens his eyes, stares at* OTTO.) He has a curious effect on a house, you know. Might as well warn you. (*Pause.*) It isn't quite a smell. It isn't quite a vibration. But you get the feeling that objects — walls and chairs and tables and things. That objects know he's there. (*Pause.*) And they don't like it. (*Pause.*) A sort of shudder of distaste goes through a house when Hugh walks in. (*Pause.*) Have you noticed it over there yet?

He rises and crosses to the window. He stands looking across the street.

He's tacking a sheet across the lavatory window.

OTTO. At least, Edward —

Pause.

EDWARD. Yes?

OTTO. I have taken him on.

EDWARD. Professionally?

Pause.

OTTO. I don't exactly know what I am doing. (*Pause.*) I — I was so moved today. When he appealed to me.

EDWARD. I expect that's what he did with Marna. Is that what you were Marna? Moved? (*Pause.*) Yes. That must be it. You were moved. And subsequently he moved in. It looks to me as if that's the way old Bainbridge goes about it.

Pause.

OTTO. I was moved by you when you were my patient.

EDWARD. Eh?

OTTO. By your desperation.

EDWARD. My what?

OTTO *rises, crosses to* EDWARD — *who moves away and sits.*

A long pause.

OTTO. Common enough symptoms. Terror. Panic. Sweating. Palpitations. A feeling of distance between yourself and the world. A sense of fading away. (*Pause.*) Sessions when you would curl up rigid on my couch. Like some catatonic mouse under a bell-jar. (*Pause: to* MARNA:) I used to ache with sorrow, Mrs Croft. That people must endure for no reason they could perceive — a condition which I had only known in the hands of the Gestapo. (*Pause.*) A condition which is of course . . . in every way a normal response. To the Gestapo. (*Pause.*) My sister Frieda used to make me laugh, because she would say. Sitting in her garden on a gentle summer's day. 'But where is their Gestapo? Danke sei Gott. Here in England? In London? My God after the Germany we knew, simply to live and breathe without fear is a benediction.' (*Pause.*) You will gather that in many respects my sister was an innocent and unsophisticated woman. I used to tap her cheek and remind her that one thing

Adolf Hitler did not initiate is the acute anxiety neurosis. And
Frieda thought this enormously witty. And she would fill our
glasses. Get mildly drunk. (*Pause*.) We were children when time
was running out for the Weimar Republic. Adored by our
mother. In awe of our then rich and powerful father. (*Pause*.)
Privileged. (*Pause*.) And Frieda could not forget those days.
(*He goes close to* MARNA.) Edward has never mentioned that
she owned this house too? That he bought it from her?
(*Pause*.) She practically gave it to him.

Pause.

MARNA. No. He hasn't mentioned it.

OTTO (*to* EDWARD): Well. After all. Why should you?

MARNA. Edward?

Pause.

EDWARD. Oh, absolutely. An act of desperation. Roots, you
know. Hook line and sinker. All that.

OTTO. It was to have been my own house. (*Pause*.) Where I
would bring this boy to live who was infatuated with Hugh
Bainbridge.

Pause.

MARNA. Yes. I see. I think I've had enough though.

EDWARD. Definitely a bit round the bend I was at the time. I even
went so far as to consult a psychoanalyst. You know. Terror.
Panic. Sweating. Thought the old rib-cage was bursting at the
seams and so forth. Oh God yes. Foaming at the mouth to
buy a house. Settle down. Yes. I find one gets awfully
intrigued by one's therapist. Eh? Hungry for bits and pieces of
mundane information about the swine. Just who he is, exactly.
You with me? Where he lives. What he really does for a living.
Any connections there might be with pre-Hitlerite Germany
and all that. Goodness me. The analysand — that's what these
blokes call the patient — your average analysand. Can actually
lose sleep wondering who the fuck he's got himself mixed up
with. (*Pause*.) Might be a rapist, a paedophile. Any kind of
goddamn thing at all. (*Pause*.) In secret. On the quiet. When the
last neurotic creeps out into the gathering dusk, and it's time
for a large gin and tonic and a dose of the objective external
world, so-called. (*Pause*.) Cor stone the crows. If a chap can't
buy a house from his analyst's sister without being accused of

an unresolved Oedipus Complex — eh? What on earth are we coming to?

OTTO. I think we are coming to your accusation that I betrayed you. Betrayed all my patients by what I did in going away. That it was not only grossly irresponsible conduct for someone in my profession, but an aggressive act against you personally. At such a vulnerable moment in your life. (*Pause.*) Why do you think I ceased to practice when I got to Canada? How do you think I judged myself? Driven this way and that by a boy whose very innocence was destructive. Obsessed by him. Cheated. Mocked. Despicably treated. And still — I can only say consumed. By an outrageous love that I never experienced in my life before. Because there was simply no limit to what I would have done for Rinaldo. I almost wished he would kill me so that I would have to take no more humiliations from him.

HUGH *enters.*

HUGH. What an invincible liar the Dottore is.

There is a long pause. HUGH *stands looking from one to the other.*

Yes. Awfully sorry. Been listening at the door. Had my beady eye on you all when tacking a sheet over the lavatory window. Couldn't resist popping over. (*Pause.*) Yes. Oh dear me. I suppose now you'll insist on having your key back at once. (*He flips it towards* MARNA, *who lets it fall on the floor.*) Not to mention what about my bloody case? Clearly you can't send the man on the simplest of errands. I confess I did knock back three stiff whiskies before coming over. Thought you might all of you gang up on me, I don't know why. (*He crosses to the case.*) But feeling pretty invulnerable just now, thank you very much. (*He kicks the case.*) Isn't it ghastly? I've often thought she has the taste of an old-fashioned poufter. (*Pause.*) As for Florence. I'd say the best way to take in the Uffizi Gallery is on roller skates — but you should have seen madam. Couldn't drag her out of the place.

OTTO *crosses to him.*

OTTO. About what have I lied?

HUGH. Well. There was that touching construction about just

coming back here to settle your affairs then totter off to Italy.
Alora. It won't be sleazy old Florence I can tell you that now.
But for sheer nerve. All the time you knew you'd really come
back for a peek at him. Didn't you? What a funny guilty old
shrink it is. As for you, Edward I'm ashamed of you. I don't
think I've met anybody quite so robust in the head as you are.
Hanging round the place. Watching. Making snide remarks
about all and sundry. Biding your time. And Jesus! — that
loopy smirk of yours. I have nightmares about it. (*He picks up
the case and heads for the door*.) When you knew I was
suffering the pangs of unrequited. Right from the moment I
clapped eyes on the pair of you. (*To* OTTO, *as he sets down
the case*.) They tried to pinch my taxi one night in Drury Lane.
I'd been standing there pissed and waving my arms like a
demented railway signal for half an hour. Needless to say
they'd been to the Royal Shakespeare. Catch me wasting my
time on a play with a title like Corioanus.

OTTO. Hugh. Stop it.

HUGH. I swear to God that's how they picked me up. She was
damned if she was going to let that cab whisk me off to
Paddington. And anyway I'd missed the last train to Oxford —

OTTO. I beg you. Please —

HUGH. You don't have to beg. I'm all yours. I can't say I wasn't
shocked to the toenails standing there behind the door, but I
do need somebody. The least you can do for someone you've
shot is nurse them back to life again. And talking of
resurrection — haven't you caught on, Otto? These two are
both dead. He does give a semblance of brio at the strings of
his instrument, I'll give him that. But that's as far as it goes.
(*He snaps his fingers*.) Come. (*Pause*.) Come come come.

Pause. He takes OTTO'S *gun from his pocket and points it
at* OTTO.

HUGH. Unlike your good self, Dottore. I've never handled one of
these things in my life. Shall we go?

A long pause. No one moves. Slowly HUGH *squeezes the
trigger. There is a click only. He holds it up, staring at it.*

HUGH. It's enough to make you weep.

Pause.

OTTO. There was never more than one bullet in it.

HUGH. Well how the shit was I supposed to know?

Pause.

OTTO. I have carried it ever since I got out of Germany. (*Pause.*) With just the one bullet.

HUGH. Well. There we are. You've made an absolute bloody fool out of me again. I must say. On top of being swathed in this ridiculous bandage, it's all a bit much. How is one supposed to maintain a facade of dignity? (*He touches the bandage.*) I suppose I could strangle you with it if I ever manage to get you back across there. Really. One way and another it's beginning to feel like the night those looney Dutchmen took his cello to Singapore. (*He goes to pour himself a drink.*) Really. For Christ's sake. I mean to say. I sometimes think I inhabit an entirely different universe from other people.

HUGH has his back to MARNA as he gets the drink. She springs at him, landing on his back like a cat out of a tree. They go down together, thrashing and flailing. HUGH tries to curl up. She kneels astride him sobbing and pummelling. EDWARD and OTTO watch. They are immobile, almost hypnotised.
MARNA rolls off HUGH to kneel panting on all fours.
HUGH is more outraged than hurt. He gets to his feet, dusts himself down, adjusts his bandage. He grabs the suitcase and goes out.
OTTO crosses to MARNA. He puts his hands out.

OTTO. Mrs Croft —

Pause.

MARNA. Marna.

OTTO. Marna —

She takes his hands. He helps her to her feet. They stand holding hands a moment. She disengages hers and turns away. She sits.

MARNA. I want to laugh.

OTTO. Then you should laugh.

Pause.

MARNA. It's only hysteria.

Pause.

OTTO. Only?

MARNA. Don't start on me.

Pause.

OTTO. No.

MARNA. Look at my husband.

OTTO looks.

The first time we went to Hugh's place in Oxford. That's how he looked. That's how he sat. When Hugh and I went upstairs together. (*Pause: she goes to pour a drink.*) You might think it indecent to talk like this about someone in their presence. But he's indifferent. (*Pause.*) He can sit anything out. He wasn't asleep when you and I came in. (*Pause.*) I knew. That's why I spoke about him and his music. That can make him stir. (*She drinks.*) Personally I'd say he's unanalysable. If there is such a word. You must have found him a challenge, did you? (*Pause.*) I used to bring my lovers here when he was giving a concert. Or practising somewhere. Or recording. It started quite soon after we were married. (*Pause.*) Then. Almost imperceptibly. We got to the point where it was an unspoken assumption that he knew what was going on. (*Pause.*) Then we began to refer to it. Obliquely. Almost casually. (*Pause.*) He knew they'd always leave me. That they'd eventually just — walk away. (*She drinks.*) In anger. Or frustration. Or boredom. (*Pause.*) Or sheer disbelief. Yes. The fact is that Edward and I simply amazed them one way or another. They'd never encountered such durability. (*Pause.*) For years we were the most stable pair I'd ever come across. (*Pause.*) But one afternoon. He walked in unexpectedly when it was Hugh and I thrashing about on the floor, stoned out of our wits. (*She drinks.*) Hugh was actually in mid-orgasm and not at all inclined to back off. But what did Edward do? Took out his paper. Opened it. Sat down where he is now. With the same frighteningly neutral expression he has now. And started reading out the stock-exchange prices. (*Pause.*) One has no option, in a situation like that. But to complete one's business and creep out. Which we did. I almost waved to him as I closed the door behind me. (*Pause.*) And when Hugh had gone. He very nearly killed me. Which was why we had to put the affair with Hugh on an entirely different basis from the others. (*Pause.*) My true love. A certain Belgian revolutionary.

Languishes in a Peruvian prison, Herr Doktor.

EDWARD. Paraguayan.

MARNA. There we go.

EDWARD *rises. He crosses to* MARNA; *stands looking at her with his hands in his pockets. He crouches on his haunches.*

EDWARD. I was jolly touched by your story. (*He rises, crosses to* OTTO: *stands looking at him, then* MARNA.) I once asked him during a particularly arid session on the couch. 'What if I'm lying? Consciously and deliberately.' (*Pause: he moves away to sit.*) 'What.' I said. 'What if you're psychoanalysing a pack of lies?' (*Pause.*) D'you know, that didn't faze him at all? (*Pause.*) It wouldn't make any difference, he said. (*Pause.*) Now what do you make of that? It knocked me for six I can tell you. I'll bet it has you stumped. It has me. (*Pause.*) It had me at the time. (*Pause.*) I wondered at first if he'd misheard me. If maybe he thought Id said: what if I'm flying? What if you're psychoanalysing a pack of flies? (*Pause.*) I was too shy to repeat the question. I wasn't going to face being told it'd make no difference if I was flying. Not lying there on his couch, I wasn't. Not spreadeagled in a normal field of one earth gravity. (*Pause.*) Can you imagine the effect on the therapist of the patient rearing up on one elbow. Screwing his pitiful head round. And saying: 'Excuse me, I did not say I was flying?' (*Pause.*) That was the day I decided to find out who the shit I was dealing with. By God yes. Ran him to earth in no time. Place of birth. Schools. University. Family tree. (*Pause.*) Philosophers and medical men swarming about in that tree like monkeys. All over Europe. Vienna. Prague. Budapest. You name it. (*Pause.*) I was dazzled. By the Lord Harry, I thought. If any chap can reconcile id, ego and superego — it's this bloke. Yes. No more moaning and groaning. No more snide cracks at the doctor from Edward Croft. Buckle down to it. Give this shrewd German a fair crack of the whip. (*Pause.*) At which point he breezed off to Canada leaving me to the tender care of one Doctor Bernard C. Glossop. Who I caught picking his nose and scratching his balls during the very first session. (*Pause.*) Well. What would you have done? (*Pause.*) I'd winkled out Frieda Neumann's address. (*He points at the window.*) I grabbed a taxi to that very house. Pointed out at some length. 'It isn't, Miss Neumann', I said. 'A question of whether psychoanalysis works or whether it doesn't. Whether

the theory is true or false. Or the practice effective or futile.'
(*Pause*.) 'It's the question of your brother turning out a
morally depraved person. As witness his criminal abandonment
of me when I'm running about in this world like a beheaded
chicken. It's unethical. It's inconceivable. It's this and that and
the other. I ask you. In the name of the dead and dispossessed
of Europe. Gnädiges Fräulein. Give me your brother's address
in Canada so I can just pop over there and do him in. It will be
a service to mankind.'

He goes to the drinks, pours one.

EDWARD. Ah, she was an impressive lady. (*Pause*.) Moving out
at the time. Leasing the place to the excruciating Denham.
(*Pause*.) She made me a cup of tea. Showed me her album of
family photos. (*He drinks*.) Fantastic one of Otto in rompers
on Oskar Kokoschka's knee. The Grünewald, the Schwarzwald,
the this that and the other wald. (*Pause*.) She totally ignored
everything I had to say about Otto. Stuffed me solid with
cheesecake. Got me blind drunk on chilled hock. Sold me this
house. Wrote me a letter of introduction to Hans Koenig.
Simply refused to believe I couldn't play the cello any more.
(*Pause*.) 'If you are brave enough to try with Hans and Polly
Koenig', she said. 'You will soar. You will play like an angel.'
(*Pause*.) Led me out blinking and staggering into the
twilight. Hailed a taxi. Actually saw me back to the flat.
(*Pause*.) The poor old bird's insane, I thought. An angel herself,
but lulu. Morally organised her life in some other dimension.
(*He drinks*.) But when she dropped me off. She said: 'I hope
you will buy the house across the street. You must write me a
very small cheque. And arrange a mortgage.' (*Pause*.) 'And
make your life there.' (*Pause*.) Then as the taxi pulled away
she leaned out and said: 'It was to have been Otto's.'

*There is a long silence. OTTO goes to MARNA and kisses her
hand. He goes to EDWARD and puts his hands on his shoulders.
They look at each other. OTTO kisses him on both cheeks and
goes out.*

MARNA crosses to the window.

MARNA. There's a crack of light in the sky. (*Pause*.) It's going
to be a hot day. I can feel it.

A pause. She raises the window sash.

EDWARD. Polly and I used to sit up half the night sometimes.
(*Pause*.) Did you and Jean-Jacques?

MARNA. I don't think we had a whole night together. (*Pause*.) Not once.

Pause.

EDWARD. I don't feel like going up, anyway.

Pause.

MARNA. I don't.

Pause.

EDWARD. I expect we shall go on till one of us dies.

MARNA. I expect so.

EDWARD. But all these years. I've watched myself in horror. In despair. (*Pause*.) Such a long procession of years. (*Pause*.) With the most unaccountable longings and yearnings. As if there were some other Edward waiting to be born. Waiting for a signal to exist. (*Pause*.) An absolutely bloody magnificent new self. A creature of humility and light. Of love. A person of exemplary tenderness and compassion.

Pause.

MARNA. I know what you mean.

EDWARD. But of course there isn't. Is there?

MARNA. No.

EDWARD. Nor in you?

MARNA. No.

Pause.

EDWARD. Polly was that sort of creature.

MARNA (*turns slowly*). Was she?

EDWARD. Was Jean-Jacques?

A pause. She turns back towards the open window.

MARNA. They're going to bed together.

EDWARD. Old Hugh didn't smash those binoculars for nothing.

Pause.

MARNA. Lights out.

EDWARD *moves closer to the window. He looks out.*

EDWARD. Italy —

Pause.

MARNA. Shall we go somewhere for a bit?

Pause.

EDWARD. We've certainly been through it.

MARNA. How Hugh must have hungered for a man.

Pause.

EDWARD. Which one of them. Do you think. Will carve up the other?

Pause.

MARNA. I hope neither. (*Pause.*) Will you switch the lights off?

EDWARD *does so. He crosses back to the window; touches her arm.*

EDWARD. Will you hold me?

Pause.

MARNA. Will you hold me?

They slowly embrace. He rests his cheek against her head.

MARNA. Will you play for me?

Pause.

EDWARD. Here and now?

MARNA. Here and now.

EDWARD. Rouse the neighbours?

Pause.

MARNA. Please? (*Pause.*) Quietly?

He goes out. MARNA sits in a chair by the window. Looking out, she waves.
EDWARD returns with the cello and sets it up.

MARNA. Hugh just opened their window. Stark naked.

Pause.

EDWARD. Did you wave?

MARNA. Yes.

Pause.

EDWARD. Did he wave back?

Pause.

MARNA. Yes.

Pause.

EDWARD. Bit of a loser, old Bainbridge.

Pause.

MARNA. Right from the start.

EDWARD *starts playing.*

Slow fade.

Curtain.